ADOPTED CHILDREN
AT HOME AND AT SCHOOL

British Agencies For
Adoption and Fostering
11 Southwark Street
London SE1 1RQ

ADOPTED CHILDREN AT HOME AND AT SCHOOL

The integration after eight years
of 116 Thai children
in the Dutch society

Prof. Dr. R.A.C. Hoksbergen
F. Juffer (M.A.)
B.C. Waardenburg (M.A.)
with the kind co-operation of
G. van de Klippe (M.A.)

SWETS & ZEITLINGER B.V. / LISSE
1987

ADOPTIECENTRUM
Rijksuniversiteit te Utrecht
Sociale Wetenschappen
Heidelberglaan 1
3584 CS UTRECHT

CIP-GEGEVENS KONINKLIJKE BIBLIOTHEEK, DEN HAAG

Hoksbergen, R.A.C.

Adopted children at home and at school : the integration
after 8 years of 116 Thai children in the Dutch society /
R.A.C. Hoksbergen, F. Juffer, B.C. Waardenburg ; [transl.
from the Dutch]. - Berwyn : Swets North America ; Lisse :
Swets & Zeitlinger. - Tab., graf.
Vert. van: Adoptiekinderen thuis en op school : de
integratie na acht jaar van 116 Thaise kinderen in de
Nederlandse samenleving. - Lisse : Swets & Zeitlinger,
1986. - Met lit. opg.
ISBN 90-265-0845-X
SISO 323.5 UDC 316.45.052-058.865 (= 1.593-82) (492) NUGI 716
Trefw.: adoptie ; buitenlandse kinderen ; Nederland.

Foto's: Femmie Juffer, Utrecht
Tekstverwerking: Selection Tekstverwerking, Leiden
Gedrukt bij Offsetdrukkerij Kanters B.V., Alblasserdam
Copyright © 1987 R.A.C. Hoksbergen en Swets & Zeitlinger, B.V., Lisse

ISBN 90 265 0845 X

CONTENTS

FOR GUIDANCE

LAND OF THE SMILE

Thailand is called the land of the smile. A typification to which those that have been there will eagerly subscribe. The Thai themselves are wont to call their country Muang Thai, the country of the free people. Freedom, too, is an important characteristic: Thailand is the only country in that part of the world that has never been colonized by a western country.

In other parts of the Third World, love of freedom and self-consciousness sometimes cause a country to take a deprecatory view of intercountry adoption, in spite of the fact that many children would be considered serious adoption candidates. Not so in Thailand: after a first phase —from circa 1971 until 1979; adoptions, described in this investigation, date back to that period— adoptions were temporarily stopped because the government had lost its grip on the course of events and numerous scandal stories were going around. Adoptions were brought to a stop, a measure was taken to put affairs in order and to make a new and better start later on. In 1980, an adoption law was enacted. The preparations for the enforcement took the authorities a considerable amount of time. Since, moreover, new regulations required a long procedure, it was not until 1984 that new Thai children started arriving in Holland via BIA/WC.

The Ministry of Public Welfare now keeps a firm control over things. They only work with reputable foreign organizations —and in principle with one organization to a country only— and, luckily, the situation whereby parents —walking through a room with small beds— were allowed to choose a child, no longer exists.

BIA has co-operated enthusiastically with the investigation of Utrecht University into the integration of Thai children who came to Holland in the seventies. It is the first study to find out to what extent and in which way the integration in Dutch society takes place of a group of children from another continent. We hope and expect that more simular studies will follow. The results could prove to be of essential importance to BIA. On the one hand for further improvement of the intermediary work and the preparation of the parents, on the other hand as a presentation —with an English transla-tion— to the Thai authorities and institutions for the care of children. The value of such a presentation should not be estimated: the countries of origin are watching the fates of their children more and more critically. Apart from the usual follow-up —condensed periodical reports on each individual child— now collected and revised investigation results will become available, which give a broader and more profound picture of the situation.

The results of the study prove over and over that an adopted child's chances are the best when it enters the adoptive family as young as pos-sible, preferably before it is six months old. An ideal situation that nowadays is practically beyond feasibility. What is more, due to procedure rules and troubles in the countries of origin, particularly in Thailand, waiting periods for the children are getting longer and longer, a situation that BIA considers rather alarming and that is essentially to the detriment of the adopted child.

The results of the investigation are based on interviews with parents and teachers. It will be clear that we nevertheless are looking forward to the announced follow-up investigation, to be held under the (now still too young) adopted children themselves: a necessary addition if the picture is to be complete. On the whole, the investigation presents a positive picture of the families with Thai children. The children themselves, too, emerge positively: vital, eager to learn, of a positive social behaviour. Qualities that will be useful to them later on, as members of society. For, like everybody else, they, too, will primarily have to search and conquer their place within that society under their own power. I wish them and their parents a good future. And, to quote a Thai proverb, you do not know your happiness until you receive it.

R.G. Deibel (MA)
President of the Netherlands Intercountry
Child Welfare Organisation.

PREFACE

Adoption of a child from a far country has become a well-known phenomenon over the past 20 years in Europe, Australia, the USA and Canada. We might even go so far as to say that foreign adoption has developed into an accepted social phenomenon. Many factors are responsible for this situation. On the one hand, we might point out the extent to which the transfer of the children to the West takes place. Although precise sum totals are lacking, an estimate of between 15.000 and 20.000 children a year does not seem far beyond the mark.

Many interesting books, reports and articles were published. More often than not, however, they tended to be rather vague, especially those that were issued in Holland. Hardly surprising, for preparatory to theoretical approaches, a new phenomenon has to be described properly. However, now that children from various countries have been living in our country for 10 years or more, we are now at the stage that we need more specific analyses.

More and more, for instance, the question presents itself as to how, considered over a longer period, the integration of these foreign adopted children into Western cummunities proceeds and by what factors it is influenced. In the present report we give an account of such an investigation. A first analysis of a group of 116 Thai children adopted in Holland in the years between 1974-1979 and their parents (88) provided us with a wealth of data. More investigations will follow.

Collecting the many necessary data would have been impossible without the open and intensive contributions of 88 of the 91 couples with an adopted child born in Thailand, and without the contributions of the teachers of various primary schools. We would like to render special thanks to them all. We also received much help from Mrs. E. van den Hazel, former agent of the Bureau for Inter-Country Adoption in Thailand, Mrs. A.B.M. Loenen (MA) and many students from various universities and disciplines.

The co-operation with the organizations World Children, Dutch Society for Inter-Country Adoption and Child Welfare and more specifically her BIA foundation, was excellent.

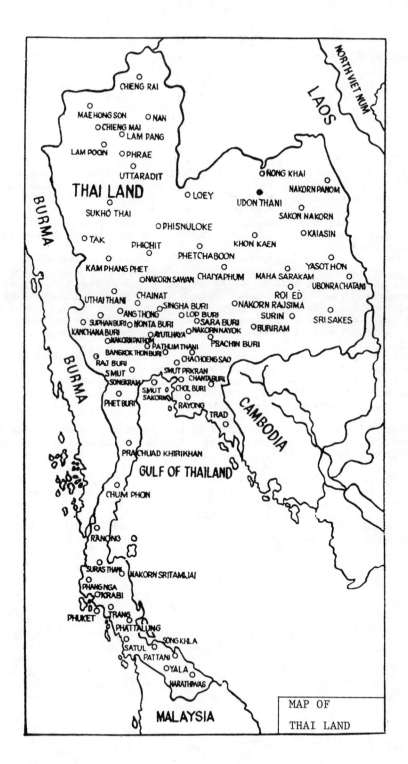

MAP OF
THAI LAND

PRELUDE

A. Thailand (1)

Thailand is a remarkable country in South-East-Asia. Lying in the midst of countries that seem to be in a perpetual state of war, from which situation Thailand suffers much inconvenience in its borderlands, the kingdom of Thailand has a relatively calm and stable social climate.

The Thais originally came from South-China and the Chinese influence is still very distinct in many fields, for instance in the very important civil codes in social contacts.

Though, as a constitutional monarchy, Thailand is not troubled by constant changes in power, it nevertheless has serious problems. Let us focus on the number of inhabitants for a start. This tripled over the last 40 years and Thailand now has ± 50 million inhabitants. The development of the necessary arrangements however, has not kept step with the explosive population growth. There is much poverty and this is one important reason why it is not possible to provide all children with sufficient care and schooling.

Another important element of Thailand is the Buddhist religion, that focuses on the individual well-being. Consequently, not much attention is paid to the common good. This means that paupers, even if they are children, are left to solve their economic problems for themselves.

Poverty and Buddhism are two factors that explain the presence of so many children in need in Thailand. The Buddhist philosophy of life also explains why adoptive families in Thailand are so hard to find. Adoption by families does take place, but a considerable number of children do not even come up for it.

B. The Children's Background

As in other developing countries that lack the means of providing all children with sufficient scope for development of their talents, there are a number of reasons why in Thailand children are offered as candidates for adoption. In Thailand poverty is the most important reason for giving up one's children. In addition, there are a few other reasons that more or less have to do with the notions of the Thais. Van den Hazel and Strijbosch (1986) review this in their thesis.

- In Thailand certain prevalent notions can cause parents to part with their newly born baby. People believe, for instance, that twins bring bad luck (2). It is also believed that a curse rests on a baby whose mother dies in childbirth. The child is considered guilty of its mother's death and, at best, is offered as a candidate for adoption.
- Children that have one or two leprous parents are usually living, with their parents, in secluded leprosy villages where conditions are primitive. Lepers have few rights, even their civil rights can be taken from them. These children's scope for development is extremely small. They

never come up for further study or a public office, even if they themselves are perfectly healthy. This often induces their parents to part
with their child.
- In the large cities, especially in the capital Bangkok, many children of
prostitutes are parted with, because their mothers are unable to sustain
the child.
- After the expulsion of American soldiers from Thailand, a number of the
children that had been fathered by them, (so-called Red-Heads) were
treated as outcasts by society.
- Due to the guerilla-activities in the Thai border countries with Laos,
Cambodja and Vietnam, many Thais were killed and many Thai children became
war orphans.

From which parts of Thailand do the children that were adopted in Holland
during the seventies come? We see that four regions in the north and middle
of Thailand are the main suppliers of adoptive children (see chart). In Udon
Thani, children are mainly parted with out of poverty, after the decease of
one or both parents, or as a result of superstition.

In Khon Kaen the situation is totally different. Here, children are
living with their parents in a leprosy colony. Because the invalidity of the
parents keeps them from taking care of their own children, or because they
want to provide a better future for their child, adoptive families are much
in demand. The population of children's homes in Bangkok is largely made up
of children of prostitutes who, more often than not, arrive there in
infancy.

All these children have been living in a children's home for a few months
or a few years after separation from their mother or parents. These children's homes are far from perfect. The description Van den Hazel gives of the
children's homes visited by her (3) illustrates not only the material, but
also the affective neglect these children are exposed to. It is chiefly
through lack of money that the managers of the children's homes more often
than not are unable to provide their children with good accomodation and
sufficient food. More smarting, however, (though luckily not everywhere) is
the lack of loving care and attention.

C. **The Dutch parent(s) in Thailand**

Before 1980, when the "Child Adoption Act" came into force, the legislation
for foreign adoption was far from clear. The Department of Public Welfare in
Bangkok had formulated a number of adoption terms, for instance that
adoptive parents were not to be younger than 30 and had to be at least 15
years older than the child and capable of maintaining a family as well. It
was, however, behind the back of the Department of Public Welfare, in the
town-halls to be precise, that the actual arrangements were made.

In almost all cases of adoption by Dutch married couples, at least one of
the biological parents was known and was obliged to come to the town-hall in
order to sign a contract of disposal. This took place in the presence of the
adoptive parents. In this way, a direct meeting between adoptive parent(s)
and biological parent(s) took place, a situation that is usually avoided in
many other adoption countries. For many parents this was a difficult moment,
partly due to the formal atmosphere of the meeting, in which there was no
room for any personal contact. More often than not, the official arrangement
was the only moment that biological and adoptive parents met.

There was yet another respect, in which the situation in Thailand

differed somewhat from that in other countries. Usually, the adoptive parents already know one or two things about the child they will adopt. It often happens that they receive a photograph and short description of their child a few weeks or months in advance. In the case of adoption of Thai children, however, the parents usually knew nothing, until they actually met the child. In our opinion, the stories told by many parents about their first meeting with their child are remarkable.

On arrival at the children's home where they were to see their child for the first time, they and other Dutch couples, would be brought to a room in which the children were either laying or sitting up in their beds. The parents then expected to be brought to the bed of "their" child, but, much to their surprice, would be asked to choose one themselves. Actually, this routine never caused any serious problems and, as far as we know, it never happened that two couples chose one and the same child. According to the parents, it often was the child itself that directed the choice: the reason for choosing that one particular child was often the feeling that it reached to them in a special way. Yet, most parents considered this an unpleasant way of meeting. They had the awkward feeling that they were being asked to see and compare and, although they did not relish it, there was little else they could do at that moment. Moreover, the situation made them painfully aware of the fact that certain children were not, and perhaps would never be, chosen and this gave rise to feelings of guilt.

The reason for Thailand to practically close its frontier to adoption in 1980, for the most part lay in the feeling of the Thai government of having absolutely no grip whatsoever on the adoption practices. This in connection with a number of incidents, in which there was talk of traffic in children. With the 1980 Child Adoption Act, all adoptions became supervised by the Department of Public Welfare. In 1984, contacts with the Thai authorities in the matter of adoption were renewed. In 1984 and 1985 some children from Thailand were once more adopted.

WHY THIS INVESTIGATION

1.1. Theoretical Relevance

Foreign adoption has been a subject of research in Holland since 1975. A first analysis of a descriptive nature was finished in 1979 (Hoksbergen et al., 1979). Since then, various other questions have led to all kinds of research activities. Often, these were stimulated by adoptive parents, or organizations dealing with adoption. Gradually, however, with the progress in the scientific research in this field and the knowledge that had been gathered, a retrospective analysis of the situation of adopted children, that no longer suffered from initial adaptation problems, became a necessity.

Starting from the existing theoretical framework, we were able to formulate certain suppositions, that, when tested in practice, quite evidently proved to be relevant. We mention here one example only. Adoptive parents seem to be more uncertain about the way in which they handle their child's upbringing than other parents. In view of this fact it is extremely relevant to supply them with reliable information about important factors that might reduce the chance of problems with the upbringing of adopted children.

There has been quite an impressive amount of scientific research in the field of adopted children over the past twenty years in the USA. Due to intensive contacts with the people involved, we were allowed free access to the results.

1.2. Practical Relevance

We first of all wanted to evaluate the situation of a group of adopted children that were born in Asia (where most foreign adopted children come from), and that had been living in Holland for a considerable number of years. Of a group, too, that was relatively homogeneous where country of origin, age and manner of placement were concerned. The Thai group, that happened to fit in where size was concerned, met these criteria. Moreover, a combined action of the adoption organizations concerned, the BIA in The Hague and the then agent in Thailand, made it possible to trace all adoptive families. We started from the supposition that this involvement would have a highly positive effect on the willingness of the adoptive parents to co-operate. Much to our relief, this supposition proved correct afterwards (chapter 3).

Many applauded this evaluation of a commendable group where matters of research were concerned. First of all, all adoption organisations, adoptive parents and candidate adoptive parents. What is more, over the past few years, Dutch society has been showing signs of a growing need for a first extensive evaluation. Just consider the various wild stories about adoption that appeared (and still appear) in the media. These stories, whether they are of the cakes and ale or grief and sorrow type, tend to have a great

on public opinion with regard to a subject that decidedly has controversial characteristics. For this reason, there is a great need in many adoptive families for systematically and carefully gathered information about matters such as problems with upbringing in adoptive families, assimilation possibilities for the children into the community, chances of discrimination, effects of neglect etc. In short, knowledge that can be put to good use.

There is yet another reason why this investigation is relevant for children in Thailand. After adoptions from Thailand to Holland had come to a stillstand in 1980, they gradually got going again in 1984 for a number of reasons. Contacts with the local authorities show that in Thailand there is a great need of information about how these children are doing in our community. Would foreign adoption, provided of course that certain fundamental conditions are satisfied, be temporarily acceptable? An answer to this important question to Thai authorities can only be given by means of research among children that have been adopted from Thailand.

Research, such as the one under consideration, is of great importance to Dutch adoption organizations, too, because it may yield information that might influence procedures at home and abroad. Or, formulated more clearly: all kinds of data that eventually may be in the interest of children in need and adoptive parents in whatever country, always deserve to be gathered. A new phenomenon naturally gives rise to numerous questions on the part of the social workers, psychologists and pedagogues involved. Answering them partly or completely will lead to an improvement of, for instance, information to the adoptive parents, the manner of placement of children and the aftercare. There is a final and more general reason. About adoption, as we said before, much is being written in the media and not only because it is considered controversial by some. It is especially the fundamental character of adoption that causes this interest. After all, it concerns moving a child (at least in the case of foreign adoption) over large distances and allowing it to be brought up by others than the natural parents. It is about a way of establishing a family and central human needs, i.e. the need of being allowed to raise children. Hardly surprising therefore, that stories about adoption in the media will attract the attention of the general public. Yet, the more people are interested in these stories, the more it is necessary to act carefully and discreetly. We should bear in mind that we are dealing with deep-rooted interests of children and parents. In the case of children from Asia, Africa and South-Amercia, moreover, we should realize that their adoption status is obvious to anyone. Another reason, therefore, especially in view of our foreign adopted children, to proceed carefully, to prevent a situation whereby their status and outward appearance alone will give rise to prejudices or ideas and expectations preconceived. To prevent the growth of a new form of discrimination for adoptive families, a form that, for the time being, we will denote as discrimination of upbringing, with unpleasant consequences for children as well as parents. Adoptive parents sometimes seem to be outlawed where it concerns the meddlesomeness and inclination of others to make all kinds of remarks about their children's upbringing, without realizing how annoying this must be to adoptive parents. Often, all kinds of press reports lead to this. All the more reason, therefore, to counterbalance all this with scientifically valid arguments.

SOME THEORETICAL SPECULATIONS

2.1. Fanshel's Study

Over the past few decades, children whose race differs from that of their parents, the so-called inter-racial adoptions, have been the subject of various studies. Well-known is Fanshel's (1972) study of the adaptation of 96 children of Indian origin that had been adopted by white American families. This adaptation, investigated over a period of successive years, was judged by data about five life domains: medical situation, cognitive ability, personality and patterns of behaviour, social relations, family relations. We would like to expand on the research into these life domains, because they provided us with a relevant framework.

Medical Aspect
Other studies, such as that by Raynor (1970) and Jackson (1976), wholly or partly adopted Fanshel's method, often omitting the medical aspect. The latter probably because of the absence of remarkable deviations in the adopted children's physical development and health. In this respect, Fanshel's findings are clearly positive too. Yet, earlier research carried out by us (Hoksbergen et al., 1979) proved that adopted children more often than not come to their adoptive parents with all kinds of medical problems, often of a serious nature. But that these medical problems almost always disappear rapidly and usually completely. Obviously all of this depends on the kind of disturbance or the nature of the affection. What cannot be disregarded, moreover, is the fact that these children come from the tropics. Sometimes, the children that are a bit older, are suffering from tropical diseases that are fairly unknown to the ordinary pediatrician or general practitioner in our country.

Cognitive Ability
The second domain mentioned by Fanshel unfailingly forms part of a general evaluation of the situation of adopted children. Sometimes the IQ's of the children that are a bit older are compared with each other, or with those of other children (Skeels, 1966; Tizard & Rees, 1977; Bunjes, 1980). Usually, however, comparisons estimating the cognitive functioning are based on school results. This is relatively easy because the investigation can be carried out in school classes, whereby the reference group is present at the same time. The advantage of comparing adopted children with children that attend the same school is that a certain equality in socio-economic setting is reached for the group as a whole.

An important reason for research at school and comparisons with class mates or peers lies in the conclusion that in our community schooling is a very important factor in establishing the integration chances of juveniles. How the child is doing at school is a question that is so often asked and so obvious that one cannot avoid answering it in evaluation studies dealing with adopted children. Finally, the youths attend various schools during a period of 10, 20 or even more years. How they are doing there and the extent

to which they feel at home are factors that contribute to their well-being in considerable measure. Likewise, the perception of their schoolsituation and the scope for their abilities it offers will greatly influence the rest of their behaviour and development.

In the case of the foreign adopted children there is yet another aspect to be considered. These children have often suffered from neglect, emotionally as well as physically. The question to be answered is to what extent this neglect has an effect on the cognitive ability. Can there be a complete recovery? Basically, the latter is hard to find out, because the comparison will always be with other children and never a comparison of the children with themselves. Yet, one can attempt to answer this question by means of a comparison of the adoption group with matched groups: children from a Third World country with an equally unhappy start in life that are not adopted and children growing up in the receiving country with socio-economically and psychologically comparable parents. Evidently, such an experiment would be impossible for ethical reasons. In a way, we would be dealing with a natural experiment.

The results of the study of Winick, Meyer and Harris (1976) seem to justify the conclusion that, after a period of malnutrition of ± 1,5 year, children, compared as a group with other children, will practically fully recover when they come to live in better circumstances over a longer period of time. Only in the case of the original underfed group does recovery seemingly fail to be complete.

Behaviour

The third life domain mentioned by Fanshel: personality and patterns of behaviour, has less often been investigated for foreign adopted children. First and foremost, this is due to the fact that quite a number of studies focus on the adaptation of adopted children at an early age. Sometimes a score is obtained on some features of behaviour, but one can hardly speak of measurement of the "personality". Moreover, in many countries the phenomenon of inter-racial adoption is only 10 - 15 years old, a fact which seriously impedes the investigation of some questions or even makes it impossible. In short, contrary to the first two life domains we briefly referred to, we cannot as easily draw on the experiences of other research. There is, however, one exception.

This concerns the question as to whether there are special problems involved in the development of children's identity. Problems that call for a special approach in education. Sorosky, Baran and Pannor (1975, 1978) conclude, on the basis of studies of identity problems among locally and inter-racially adopted children, that many adopted children, especially during the adolescence period between 12 - 18 years, are constantly occupied with the basis of their existence. They suffer from a sense of isolation and alienation that is caused by the break in the continuity of the consecutive generations. Various other investigations (e.g. Triseliotis, 1973; Jaffee & Fanshel, 1970) prove that there is a connection between this preoccupation with the past and the quality of the relation with the adoptive parents. There is little ground for the supposition that this will be different for foreign adopted children.

Whatever the case, from what has gone before it may be concluded that an evaluative study among adopted persons during, or directly after, the adolescence phase has to investigate development of identity as an aspect of personality building.

Measuring the percentage of adopted persons that seek help or apply at a clinic for psychiatric help or at a similar institution, is another way of finding out facts about the personality building of the adopted (Rathbun, 1965). Although the percentages mentioned often vary a great deal, one may nevertheless usually conclude that the adopted are relatively overrepresented (Van Buuren, 1983). Apparently, the adopted are more susceptible to emotional disturbances and more inclined to maladjusted behaviour. These studies are often criticized for their failure to consider the selection criteria that might influence the reasons why the parents do or do not call in help from others.

Remarkable too, is the fact that no mention is made of the frequent occurrence of maladjusted behaviour in the school situation. All the more reason, therefore, to conclude that a clear and complete picture of the effect of intercountry and inter-racial adoption can only be obtained through studies that are longitudinal and that take account of the original situation of the adopted children.

Relations
In many studies much attention is paid to the last two life domains mentioned by Fanshel (Gill & Jackson 1983; Feigelman & Silverman 1983: Jewett 1978) whereby the ability to establish relations is the central issue. Particularly the question as to how relations are established within the family, is of overall fundamental importance to adoptive parents. In fact, what is at stake here, is the well-being of the family and the possibility of establishing a normal parent-child relation.

On the basis of an estimate of the number of unsuccessful adoptions (the child is removed from the first adoptive family once and for all) one sometimes goes so far as to make a very general statement about the degree of success of adoption (Hoksbergen 1983). Other important subjects are establishing relations with other children in the family, and the effects of neglect. Especially the latter has hardly been investigated for older children. This is partly due to the fact that it is difficult to reliably operationalize the concept of attachment for older children.

Various studies have also investigated the adopted children's establishment of relations at school and in the neighbourhood with peers. On the whole, the results of these studies are not very remarkable. Perhaps, an exception has to be made for the inter-racially adopted children that enter the school situation with clear signs of neglect, or make contact with peers in other ways (Bunjes 1986).

2.2. Guide for this Study

The life domains mentioned by Fanshel and the consecutive investigation have been important bases for our questions. Important, too, was the extensive and long experience in our clinical practice with regard to all kinds of problems of adoptive parents and adopted children. Finally, the results of the various investigations we carried out among families with adopted children have been very helpful, too.

Due to the available knowledge, we were able to formulate clear hypotheses on a number of facts, hypotheses that deserve to be tested. For reasons of readability and convenience of reference we will expand on this in the discussion of the various results in the following chapters. We knew from data that were available beforehand that practically all children were too young to be in the adolescence phase. However, the neccesity of research into the specific problems of families with foreign adopted children has been urged by various people (e.g. Boeke, 1978).

We know from our clinical practice that a number of specific questions crop up among adopted children in this period of their life. For this reason we were looking for a group that would qualify for longitudinal research. A group that we might follow over a longer period of time. The "Thai-group" fitted well within this framework. There is yet another reason why we set up and carried out the investigation along these lines. In the Adoption Centre, we are in the process of setting up an extensive investigation, in co-operation with the Tata Institute of Social Sciences in Bombay, among a large group of adopted children from India in comparison with children in India and various control groups. For this investigation we make use of certain notions of which the instrumental realization is still limited. The Thai-group enables us to test the validity of certain instruments.

The accuracy of the gathered data was safeguarded by the high demands that were made on the people by whom the investigation was carried out (see next chapters), the method of approach of the families and teachers and by various checks on the way in which the information was gathered (e.g. double coding and punching). Certain aspects were approached in more ways than one, so that it is possible to carry out tests with regard to internal consistency.

PLAN AND REALIZATION OF
THE INVESTIGATION

3.1. Response

Thanks to our data and the co-operation of the civil registration, it was easy to retrieve the addresses of all 93 adoptive parents that had adopted a child from Thailand between 1974–1979. As it turned out, two couples had emigrated to countries outside of Europe. The other 91 couples received a letter from the Adoption Centre with a request to participate in the investigation. Only three couples refused to do this. However, we <u>did</u> contact them, either directly or indirectly, in order to learn their reasons for refusing to participate and to get them to co-operate after all. All three showed signs of a certain aversion to contacts with official bodies on the issue of their family formation. Their refusal to participate did not seem to be influenced by the situation of the adopted child. It goes without saying that we are extremely content with the response rate of 96%.

3.2. The Interview

Interviewing only the parents sufficed for the aim of this investigation. In the announced follow-up investigation, the children will be directly approached too, if possible. In view of the children's ages this will take place in a few years' time.

The interview, during which 4 other instruments were presented too, lasted between 2 and 3 hours. In almost all cases both parents were present. The subject matter of the questions made this necessary. Certain instruments were left at home to be answered in the absence of the interviewers, both, because they lent themselves to it, and because, otherwise, the investigation at home would have taken up too much time. Sending back the material did not prove problematic.

The parents were interviewed by the authors of this report. The latter are all working as lecturers for Utrecht University and have been intensively occupied with the ins and outs of adoption for many years. MA students of clinical pedagogics assisted them in recording the data. The decision that only experts in the field of adoption should be allowed to interview, was very deliberate. We know from experience that, as a rule, conversations with adoptive parents are very intensive. They usually do not hesitate to elaborate on very personal family affairs. The subject matter of the interview certainly induced them to it. They sometimes come up with concrete questions or problems that, as a researcher, one cannot ignore. What is more, going into demands for help uttered during research, happens to be the general policy of the Adoption Centre, the responsible authority. In some cases, the investigation even led to further assistance of the family during a couple of months.

3.3. The Family Dimension Scales (1)

The dimension scales used by us (FDS) are a Dutch version of the Family Adaptation and Cohesian Scales (Faces I and II) of Olson, Sprenkle and Russell (Olson et al. 1979, 1983). The questionnaire, that has to be filled in by both parents seperately, consists of 3 scales in which three family dimensions are mapped out: Family Cohesion, Family Adaptation and Social Desirability.
The Cohesion dimension consists of the poles Loose Sand (very low cohesion) and Knot (very high cohesion) and two middle levels: Individually-oriented and Collectively-oriented. The Adaptation Ability dimension consists of the poles Static (very low adaptation ability) and Chaotic (very high adaptation ability). By means of the third dimension: the Social Desirability Scale, we can gain an insight into the degree the family members are inclined to give a rosy picture of the family's actual functioning. This is indicated by an extremely high score, whereas an extremely low score points to the opposite.
The authors of this instrument collected data among other Dutch families during the same investigation period. As a result, it is possible to make comparisons and to see whether certain differences between adoptive and other families that were expected by us, actually exist. At the same time, it is possible to study the extent to which there is a relation between "the colour of the family structure" and the occurrence of certain problems regarding upbringing.

3.4. Kirk's Instrument

Studies that the American sociologist David Kirk carried out among more than 2000 locally adopted children between 1961 and 1964, use was made of an instrument to obtain an index for certain attitudes of parents (Kirk, 1981). This chiefly concerns the attitude "acknowledgement-of-difference" versus "rejection-of-difference". This indicates the way in which adoptive parents perceive their parenthood with regard to the adopted child in comparison with other parents. Do they experience this parenthood as completely similar (rejection of difference) or as different in some respects? Kirk assumes certain correlations with three other indices: the parents' empathic ability with regard to the way in which the child perceives its adoption status, the communication between parents and child about adoption, and the child's trust in its parents.

3.5. The Parents' List

The parents' list constructed by us (Loenen, 1984) is based on the "goodness of fit model" of Thomas and Chess (1980). Goodness of fit indicated the correspondence between on the one hand characteristics of the environment and expectations with regard to the child, and motivation, talents and temperament of the child on the other. If a correspondence is lacking, Thomas and Chess denote this as poorness of fit. If this is the case, the child is expected to show signs of a disturbed development or maladjusted functioning. This does not mean to say, however, that in case of goodness of fit the child's functioning will always be uncomplicated. After all, there will always be areas of tension. What is important, though, is how the people involved manage to cope with these areas of tension. A question that is particularly important to adoptive parents, who, as we know, are not in a position to become attached to the child from the moment of birth onwards. We also attempted to operationalize the concept of attachment by means of this list. For this specific purpose, we made use of a questionnaire by Barbara Tizard (1977). The parents' list provides us with information about the patterns of behaviour of the child and about the family relations. This list was filled in by the two parents seperately. As "attachment questions" form part of the interview, it is possible to verify both reliability and validity, by means of determining the correlations between the two sets of figures. We will carry out this analysis in a later phase.

3.6. Behaviour List - Child

Many foreign adopted children have a period of neglect behind them. So far, all our research points to this fact. Similar conclusions can be drawn from reports from Sweden and Germany. One often comes upon cases of "maternal deprivation", early affective neglect.

Four syndromes are connected with this form of neglect: acute discomfort, behavioural disturbances, lag in intellectual development (especially where verbal intelligence is connected) and insensitive psychopathy.

What we are trying to find out by means of our behaviourlist is most of all the extent to which one came upon and still comes upon the most important disturbances and forms of insensitive psychopathy (inability to establish relations and form ties) mentioned in literature. We expect children that were adopted at an older age to initially display problems. We expect that in most cases this problematic behaviour will disappear as a result of the dedication of the parents. Through our data, we will also be able to gain an insight into behaviour that shows less signs of recovery (Hoksbergen, 1985). The list is filled in by most important care-takers or by both parents together.

All of the preceding instruments were filled in by the parents. The next two were presented to the teachers in primary education with the consent of the parents.

3.7. The Behaviour At School Assessment List (SCHOAL) (2)

The SCHOAL is designed as an expedient for teachers in primary education. Through a systematic and detailed description of the behaviour at school they can gain a better insight into the children's socio-emotional functioning. The impressions about the pupils' concrete and perceptible behaviour are determined by the teachers afterwards.

The scale has 4 sub dimensions: Frankness (12 comments), Attitude towards Work (12 comments), Social Contact (10 comments) and Emotionality (8 comments). We use this instrument in order to try and gain an insight into the psycho-social functioning of the child in comparison with its classmates. For this reason, data of two classmates (boy and girl) were collected for each child. Considering the surplus character of the adoptive parents, we expect that the group as a whole will have a higher score on Attitude towards Work and Social Contact. The other two dimensions cannot be described in terms of good and bad.

3.8. The Teacher's Questionnaire

The teacher was asked to judge the child's level of achievement in the various subjects, on the basis of the schoolmarks obtained. At the same time, some items were added, partly as a verification of questions that were asked elsewhere. The main aim of this list is to establish the cognitive functioning of the child according to the teacher. We will be able to find out whether deprived children's verbal faculties really are not up to the mark.

At the same time, it will be possible to find out to what extent the child is considered to be a "problematic pupil" by the teacher in comparison with its classmates and as far as concentration is concerned.

CHARACTERISTICS OF THE
ADOPTIVE FAMILIES

4.1. Family Structure at the Moment of Investigation and during the Placement of the Child

In 1984, 88 adoptive parents with at least one child from Thailand were willing to participate in our investigation. We consider the non-response of 4% negligible for the rest of the observations. The investigation concerns a total of 116 children. In 28 families 2 children from Thailand were adopted, in 4 cases these were twins.

Table 4.1. shows that 75% of the families have adopted children only, in some cases as many as 4. Compared with national data, there are slightly more children per family on an average. Also, our group convincingly comes to the general standard of 2 children per family. In 8% of the families there is only one child, which is considerably below the national average.

Table 4.1. Number of adopted- and own children, absolutely and in percentages

number of children	adopted children only	own children too 1	own children too 2 or more	total abs.	%	total Dutch %*
1	7	–	–	7	8	37
2	36	8	–	44	50	45
3	18	8	4	30	34	14
4/more	6	–	1	7	8	4
	67 (76%)	16 (18%)	5 (6%)	88	100%	100%

*) (Source: Central Statistical Office, 1984)

The family structure at the moment of placement is very important for a better understanding of the scope for the development of the children's talents (to be discussed in later chapters). The most favourable prediction for a satisfactory educational process can be made for those families where the adopted child is the first child or, if children are already present, where the adopted child is the youngest (Frederiks et al. 1984). Basically, this specific family structure is one of the criteria laid down by Dutch adoption organizations, particularly WC–BIA (1). Yet, there still are 8 (7%) above- and in-between placements in our group. In the other cases, the adopted children either were the first (65%) or the youngest child (28%).

In addition, we also determined the age difference between the adopted child and the child that comes closest where age is concerned. In 19 cases this difference is less than 2 years. This, too, is one of the criteria laid down by BIA. After all, a small age difference more often than not gives rise to such strong feelings of competition and jealousy that the adopted child's adaptation may become more problematic than necessary. An analysis of possible problematic situations within the families will therefore have to consider the family structure at the moment of placement.

4.2. Socio—economic Environment

We know from other research that adoptive parents form anything but a random group where socio-economic environment is concerned. From a career- and schooling point of view their environment is a good deal higher than what would have been expected if they had been an average group. This was obvious in our investigation, too. Usually the families' housing ranges from good to very good (60%). Only 3 families are living in modest flats. Of a similar group, made up of representatives of the entire Dutch community between 25 and 64 years of age, 21% are living in a flat. The adoptive families were mostly to be found in the shaded neighbourhoods of the cities, or in the smaller (and thus greener) towns. From a geographical point of view, the children's housing conditions are excellent.

The adoptive parents' level of schooling is markedly different from that of the average Dutch group (table 4.2.).

Table 4.2. Level of schooling of adoptive parents, compared with the Dutch
population between 35 and 54 years of age

| | MEN | | WOMEN | |
	adoption	Dutch pop.	adoption	Dutch pop.
low (up to lower vocational education)	9%	34%	20%	47%
middle	41%	46%	57%	42%
high (higher vocational education/university)	50%	20%	23%	11%

(Source: Central Statistical Office 1983)

In the adoption group, the difference in level of schooling between men and women is similar to that in the total Dutch group. On an average, the fathers' level of schooling is much higer. Hence, in this particular respect, the adoption group resembles the total Dutch group, in spite of the fact that the level of schooling of the adoption group as a whole is much higher. There is yet another respect in which this group differs from national developments. Of all 91 couples (including the non-response) only 5 couples have had anything to do with divorce. This low percentage sharply contrasts with a national group comparable qua length of marriage (18 years). The latter has a divorce percentage of about 12 (2). This low number of divorces will partly be due to the selection caused by the family investigation itself. Yet, it may very well be that the child- (and conse-quently family-) mindedness of this group is the important underlying factor. Whatever the case, fact is that we may conclude from this datum that, on the whole, adoptive families seem to be more stable. In all 5 cases of divorce the attending parent either remarried or began a lasting re-lationship.

4.3. Motivation

We know from Kirk's investigation (1981) and from earlier Dutch data
(Hoksbergen et al., 1979) that adoptive parents may globally be divided into
two groups according to their motives for adoption. The largest group
consists of couples that are strongly family-oriented in their ideas. They
like children and consider their educational task an important life fulfil-
ment. We call them internally-oriented parents. Usually, these couples are
involuntarily childless. It is a known fact that only 20% of the total group
of involuntarily childless couples (3) opt for adoption (Hoksbergen, 1979).
Then there is the group with abstract ideals. The latter refuse, for
instance, to contribute to the mondial overpopulation or are very shocked by
the difficult circumstances of many children in the Third World.

About three-quarters of our group belonged to the internally-oriented
parents, whereas a quarter belonged to the externally-oriented couples. It
will be clear that we are dealing with a rough classification here. There
are a number of very obvious differences between the two groups. There are
more involuntarily childless couples among the internally-oriented parents,
a fact that was to be expected. Also, they more often express a preference
for a younger child. Of the externally-oriented parents 17% prefer a child
over 3 versus only 2% of the internally-oriented couples.

Interesting is the fact that almost all parents gave an affirmative
answer to the question whether their motives for adoption had remained the
same over the years. The originally idealistic and abstract approach of 2
couples has become less extreme, while in the case of 4 other couples the
child itself has become more important than the parents' self-interested
longing for a child.

These slight changes in so important an aspect as motivation for adoption
give rise to the supposition that there is an intense and strong longing for
a child among the members of this group. A longing that over the years and
(possibly) in spite of all experiences within the family is not easily
changed. Other factors may also contribute to this stability. Some of these
factors will be discussed later on. We will here focus on the remarkable
fact that adoptive parents are in a position to express strong preferences
with regard to certain important characteristics. It goes without saying
that all parents that get a child will have specific preferences as to the
child's sex and general health. Adoptive parents, however, can actually
influence the realization of this preference. They are asked about their
preferences by the intermediary organizations in Holland as well as in the
country of origin. As far as our group is concerned, most preferences that
were expressed had to do with either age or sex. Other aspects, such as
health or preference for a sibling, received less explicit attention.

The most obvious conclusion that can be drawn from the answers is that
most couples, whether they adopt a first or a second child, express a
preference (85%).

Preference for Age?
What we expected, actually proved to be true. The preference expressed most
often was that for as young a child as possible (table 4.3.), in spite of
the fact that within the Thai group the number of "no preferences" is quite
considerable in comparison with other groups: 23% versus 14% or 7% (Hoksbergen, 1979).

Table 4.3. Preference for age, in case of a first, second and following child, absolutely and in percentages

age	first child abs.	%	second and fol. child abs.	%	total abs.	%
no preference	20	23	7	25	27	23
under 1	47	53	16	57	63	55
1–3	16	18	4	14	20	17
over 3	5	6	1	4	6	5
	88	100	28	100	116	100

If there already is a child in the family there is a slight shift towards "no preference" and preference for "older children". An important fact to be considered. Placing older children, in local as well as intercountry adoption, often proves much of a problem. Far fewer parents prove to be willing to adopt them. However, the couples that do opt for them often already have children. This in itself should be enough to prevent the countries of origin from formulating requirements such as 'placement of a child only takes place on condition that there is no or only one other child in the family'. Such requirements will even make it more difficult to place older children or will result in the latter's being placed with couples that would have preferred a much younger child, which would seriously impede the parent-child adaptation.

Preference for Sex?
A preference for sex is far less often expressed than a preference for age, only 34% either want a boy or a girl. If there is a strong preference on the part of the parents, this will rather be for a girl (69%) than for a boy (31%). If there already are children in the family the preference expressed is for a boy rather than for a girl. All these data correspond with results of earlier investigations carried out by us. These results show a limited preference for the adopted child's sex, too. If there is a preference at all, it will tend to be for a girl. Others have gone into the reasons for this phenomenon (Feigelman & Silverman 1983, p. 44-45). We on our part would like to once again draw attention to a fact that should be considered by the authorities responsible for the adopted children's placement. People that already have one or more children will tend to prefer a boy rather than a girl. Often this boy can be over 3. All the more reason for the organizations and authorities involved to adopt a more lenient policy where the matter of family structure is concerned.

Finally, relating the preferences expressed to the actual placements, we may conclude that the parents' wishes were satisfied to a very high extent. In three-quarters of the cases the preferences expressed were met. In those cases where this was not so, this circumstance led to hesitations on the part of the adoptive parents in 4 cases out of 25.

4.4. **Summary**

On the whole, it seems justified to conclude that the group of parents of an adopted child from Thailand is hardly different from other groups of adoptive parents. The group is strongly child-minded and, on an average, of a high socio-economic level. What the involuntarily childless couples want most of all is a young child and there is only a limited preference for sex. The latter more often for a girl than for a boy. Couples that already have children more often express a preference for a boy than childless couples.

THE PLACED THAI CHILD

This study investigates how the 59 boys and 57 girls from Thailand are doing in our country. What was necessary for a better understanding of the situation of their adoptive parents is necessary for the adopted children, too: providing more general information about the children themselves, for instance about age, health, situation in the country of origin and suchlike. Only in this way will we be able later on to gain a better insight into the reasons why certain developments took place among the 116 children. After all, part of their life story happened before they entered the adoptive family.

5.1. Age at the Moment of Placement and at the Moment of Investigation

Many investigations go into a full consideration of the effect of age at the moment of placement on further prospects for development. We, on our part, would like to pay attention to this particular aspect, too, because we know from previous research that there is a connection between the child's age at the moment of placement and various aspects of development and educational problems.

An investigation carried out at the Child Welfare Council in Amsterdam in the spring of 1985 (Hoksbergen & Van Sijl, 1985) provided us with a reasonable picture of the average age at which foreign adopted children enter Holland (1).

We figured out the average age of all children that were placed between 1970 and 1984 by the district of Amsterdam. This turned out to be almost 2 years. Earlier research of ours yielded the same result (Hoksbergen, 1979, p. 58). The children in our group, however, are remarkably younger, as is shown by table 5.1. Their average age is about 10 months.

Table 5.1. Age of Thai children at the moment of arrival, according to sex, absolutely and in percentages

age	BOYS abs.	%	GIRLS abs.	%	TOTAL abs.	%
6 months and younger	31	52	43	75	74	64
7 months - 12 months	13	22	5	9	18	15
13 months - 24 months	6	10	5	9	11	10
25 months - 36 months	4	7	2	3,5	6	5
over 36 months	5	9	2	3,5	7	6
	59	100	57	100	116	100

There are still two other aspects of time that we have to consider if we want to obtain an accurate picture of the group as a whole: the amount of time the children have been living with the family, and their age at the moment of investigation.

As for the amount of time spent with the family, all children have been living with the family for a number of years, 60% have been in Holland for 8 years or more and no child has been in Holland less than 3 years. The average length of stay is 8 years and 5 months. This relatively long length of stay was a conditio sine qua non where the matter of carrying out research among this group was concerned.

The age at the moment of investigation (see table 5.2.) ranges from 5 to 15, but the vast majority of the children belong to the primary school age group (92% are between 5,5, and 11,5 years old). The average age of the group as a whole is well over nine years.

Table 5.2. The children's age at the moment of investigation (1984) in percentages (N = 116)

age:	5	6	7	8	9	10	11	12	13	14
% :	4	6	15	22	25	16	4	5	2	1

We might say that this group is reasonably homogeneous: the same country of origin, a large number of years spent in Holland, practically all children are in the primary school age group, as many boys as girls. Obviously, we will have to pay extra attention to the time variable, because the latter might prove to influence matters such as behaviour and cognition.

It is a well-known fact that the adopted child's age may slightly differ from the one officially stated. This is partly due to the fact that it is difficult to determine a foundling's exact age, especially if the condition he is found in is poor.

In our group, the official ages proved correct in almost all cases (96%). Of the 5 children whose ages proved incorrect, one child was considerably older. In the other 4 cases, the difference between the official and actual ages was far smaller. Four of the 5 couples indicated not finding it hard to accept this fact. We may conclude from this fact that the age problem does not play an important part here.

5.2. Background information

All parents personally fetched their child from Thailand. This led to their obtaining some knowledge about their child's background in the country of origin. Often, the parents even met the person that officially parted with the child, usually the biological mother.

The parents of almost all children (there were seven exceptions) gave an affirmative answer to the question "Do you know something about your child's background?", a fact that compares favourably with data that we collected earlier (Hoksbergen, 1979, p. 60).
We then asked the parents about the nature of the information they had at their disposal. On the basis of the answers to this question we divided the children into two groups: children with and without a problematic back-ground. The term problematic stands for a situation whereby a child lived in

a children's home, or at various addresses, for three months or more. Little is known about the factors that are responsible for the problems in the children's original social environment. This can give rise to considerable feelings of uncertainty and to concrete questions on the part of the adoptive parents. Especially if the child has medical problems or behavioural disturbances. In such cases, parents would like to gain a clear insight into the possible causes of these problems, such as genetic basis, prenatal development and process of birth. A better insight may lead to a better understanding on the part of the parents as well as on the part of the assistance organizations involved. Now it is only in retrospect that conclusions can be drawn. This also holds true for our group.

In determining the nature of a child's background we should realize that the age at which the child was separated from the biological mother plays a decisive part, too. By way of precaution, we considered the group of children under 3 months at the moment of placement, non-problematic beforehand. This leaves 81 children. How many of these children have a problematic background, that is, as far as it has been made operational by us? This happens to be the case with 42 of the 81 children; institutionalization hereby plays the main part.

5.3. Some Medical Information

In order to complete the rough picture of the situation of our Thai adopted children we asked their parents about the children's health at the moment of arrival.

In collecting the medical data presented by the parents the problem that faces us is whether their view of their child's health can be trusted to be valid. Are parents at all fit to judge their child's medical condition? We think they are for the following two reasons. First of all, we are only striving for a rough picture. That was the reason why we asked questions about the children's general health (good, reasonable, poor) at the moment of arrival in Holland and about the nature of the problems. Did any important medical problems present themselves and how is the present medical situation? Considering the adoptive parents' strong involvement with their child, we think that their opinion will be reasonably valid.

The second reason is that adoptive parents usually go to their general practitioner or to a pediatrican as soon as they have returned from the country of origin, something that is strongly recommended by the intermediary adoption organizations. This happened to be the general practice in our group, too. What this means, then, is that parents, in rendering their own opinion, will also take into account the opinion of an expert.

What now was the situation of this relatively young group of children at the moment of arrival? As a matter of fact, it proved to be worse than expected. Of the parents 50% consider their child's health poor, or even bad (17%). Which problems were observed? Thirty-eight % of the children were suffering from some, sometimes serious, disease. Twenty-one % were suffering from malnutrition and two children were rather seriously handicapped. Particularly that 13 children that were over 2 at the moment of arrival were in a poor physical condition. Half of them were even considered to be in ill health by their parents. The same applied to only 14% of the other children. On the whole, the medical picture of this group is not different from that of other groups of foreign adopted children examined by us (Hoksbergen, 1979, p. 125). Considering the young age of our group at the moment of arrival, a slightly more favourable outcome would have been more in keeping with our expectations.

Considering the poor start of these children (that is, from a medical point of view), we are curious to know whether this has an effect on their further development. If a child's health condition remains poor or even bad, and new medical problems arise, this may negatively influence all kinds of aspects (cognition, relations, self-esteem). In the literature dealing with this subject, we often come upon remarks stating that medical problems among adopted children tend to disappear rather quickly, no matter how serious they sometimes may seem at first hand.

First of all, let us see whether, apart from the ordinary children's complaints, other medical problems arose later on. This happens to be the case with 40 children. Nine of them are even said to have serious problems. Considering the poor start of the children, this outcome was to be expected. It also indicates that, from a medical point of view, many parents have a tough time with their children.

The next question we came up with was whether there was a difference between children of different ages at the moment of arrival. In order to find this out, we examined the medical history of four age groups (2), from the moment of arrival onwards. The youngest children (under 6 months at the moment of arrival) came out worst, worse than, for instance, the group of children between 7 and 12 months old (or even older). Probably, however, what also plays a part in the case of these very young children is the fact that specific medical problems are hard to diagnose. The risk of disturbances, deviations and diseases manifesting themselves later on is greater in the adoption of very young babies. That this is true is also proved by the fact that now, after so many years, the health of 5 of this youngest group is still considered poor or bad by the parents. The same applies to only 1 of the other children.

If we compare the initial medical condition of our 116 children with the present situation, it may well be concluded that this group shows a remarkable recovery. Only in the case of 1 of the 20 children that were in very poor health at the moment of arrival did this opinion remain unchanged. The same goes for 5 children of the group (of originally 37) whose health was classified as poor. Hence, in the opinion of the parents, 6 children are suffering from serious medical problems. This outcome seems to justify another supposition, i.e. the idea that the children involved in foreign adoption tend to be strong and vital. What makes us think so? Mainly because of the fact that these children managed to stay alive in the country of origin under conditions that other children would never have been able to survive, and actually do not survive. After all, they often come to Holland and other Western countries under-nourished, ill and even handicapped. This goes for all children, irrespective of their age at the moment of arrival.

If this supposition of a good vitality and strong physical basis is true, it is to be expected that later on, these children will well be able to bear comparison with other children of the same age. This "later on" will have to be a good deal later, as has already been shown (table 5.2.) to be the case in our group of children. That is the reason why we asked the parents to roughly compare their child with children of the same age as to general physical development (growth, length, weight) and motor system (walking, moving, dexterity, getting dressed and suchlike) (table 5.3.).

Table 5.3. Physical and motor development of adopted children, compared with
children of the same age, absolutely and in percentages

opinion development:	PHYSICAL abs.	%	MOTOR abs.	%
ahead	10	9	36	31
no difference	90	78	69	60
behind	16	14	11	10
	116	100	116	100

The above-mentioned supposition seems to be correct. In spite of a poor
start in life, these children are doing surprisingly well from a physical as
well as a motor point of view. One would expect far more children to be
behind (3). The opposite is true. Remarkable futhermore, is the fact that
there does not seem to be a connection with the age at the moment of
arrival. The 16 children that are behind in physical development and the 11
children that are behind from a motor point of view are spread evenly over
the four age groups. Hence, from a physical point of view, it certainly is
not true that "older" adopted children cause more problems.

We should not forget, however, that we are dealing with a strongly
subjective opinion here. Both, the fact that the opinion under consideration
is that of the parents and the fact that it turns out rather positive, call
for a certain amount of suspicion. In fact, we might well ask ourselves
whether adoptive parents tend to judge their child more positively when they
compare them with other children of the same age. If there is any truth in
this suspicion, parents that consider their child ahead in development will
have an unexpectedly positive opinion with regard to other points of
comparison as well. We verified this by comparing the parents' opinion about
their child's level of achievement and language development with the opinion
of the teacher. The opinion of the parents did not prove to be more positive.

5.4. Summary and conclusions

With an average age of less than 10 months our group of children is considerably younger at the moment of arrival than adopted children from other
countries. Since all of them have been living here for a period of about 8.5
years, we may call them a settled group of children. A first evaluation of
their general adaptation, therefore, seems useful.

In comparison with other adoptive parents, the parents of these children
know a great deal about their children's background. For 50% of the children
over 3 months at the moment of arrival, this background is problematic. The
medical condition at the moment of arrival is problematic, too. In spite of
the children's relatively young age, their medical condition is considered
poor or even bad by 50% of the parents. The statement that adopted children
often are vital and strong, as appears from their recuperative power, also
holds true for our group. At present, almost all children are in good health
in comparison with other children of the same age. The supposition that the
opinion of the parents might be too positive, seems to be unfounded.

HOW ADOPTIVE PARENTHOOD
IS EXPERIENCED

The decision to raise children and to lead them to adulthood has far reaching consequences for the lives of the adults by which it is taken. It involves changes in various fields. Whatever the case, a couple (1) that gets children will for the most part end up in another position within the structure of society than a couple that remains childless. The family takes up a fundamental position within this structure. Much of the system of standards and values is determined by this family unit. It is only natural, therefore, for changes within the family to take effect in many fields of life and to receive a good deal of attention. We will give two examples that are relevant to our investigation.

The first example is of a qualitative nature and has great quantitative consequences. We are concerned with the waning influence of various ideologically tinted notions, especially religious ones, on the family. This waning influence has played an important part in the process that eventually resulted in the sexual revolution. Nowadays, more and more young people tend to live together for a number of years before getting married. This phenomenon is accepted by large groups of society. As sexuality is associated with procreation, it is only natural for changes in sexuality to immediately influence the way in which society reproduces itself. Hence, it stands to reason that the systematic character of the procreation process has become more important. If we consider this development we do not seem to be putting it too strongly when we suppose that that the births of more and more children have been planned (a development that in our opinion will have a positive effect on the national mental health). If the latter is true, the number of unwanted children must have dropped. That this actually is the case is shown by table 6.1. We would like to comment, however, that it is not entirely correct to deduce the fall in unwanted births from the number of children that were parted with, only. After all, opinions about "giving up" one's children may have changed, too. Apart from the fact that this phenomenon is not taboo any more, economic factors play an important part as well. Over the past few decades, for instance, public assistance schemes have made it easier for unmarried mothers to reasonably take care of their children where material matters are concerned.

The second important quantitative change we would like to mention is closely connected with the afore-mentioned change. The total number of births has fallen drastically in only a few years' time (6.1.) and the two-children-family seems to have become the norm.

Table 6.1. The number of adopted Dutch and foreign children and the total
number of births, 1970–1986

year	Dutch	adopted children Index	foreign	Index	Dutch-born children	Index
1970 (2)	747	100	142	100	238.910	100
1972	396	53.0	203	143	214.130	89.6
1974	214	28.6	619	436	185.980	77.8
1976	157	21.0	1125	792	177.090	74.1
1978	144	19.3	1211	853	175.400	73.4
1980	104	13.9	1594	1123	181.300	75.9
1982	77	10.3	1045	736	172.070	72.0
1984	63	8.4	1099	774	174.440	73.0
1985	72	9.6	1137	800	177.000	74.0
1986	?		1292	910	184.300	77.1

(Source: CSO, Department of Justice, Direction Child Welfare)

It will be clear that the sharp fall in the number of Dutch children that
have been given up has had much influence on the phenomenon of adoption.
Until about 1970, adoption in Holland had been almost completely "white".
Foreign children were adopted, to be sure, but most of them were of European
origin. Until 1970, the number of foreign, mainly Greek and Austrian,
adopted children was about 1.400 (3) (diagram I, next page).

Had we determined the demand for adoption on the basis of the number of
children adopted during the sixties, the outcome would not have been more
than 900 children a year. In the sixties, the phenomenon of a national
waiting list of candidate adoptive parents did not yet exist. There were
waiting lists, to be sure, but per Child Welfare Council only. In those days
the demand could be met, although even then people were warned about long
waiting periods (Nota, 1960; Mansvelt, 1967). Also, before 1972, the number
of couples turned down by the Councils was much larger. However, when at the
end of the sixties a second important change took place within the families
and, as a matter of fact, within Western society as a whole, the adoption
picture was quickly modified. This change had its roots in the fifties. What
we are talking about is the growing influence of the media in our society,
particularly that of television. In the course of the sixties, owning a
television set became as common a phenomenon among Dutch families as owning
a radio set. Naturally, the growth in prosperity contributed to this
development. When, at the end of the sixties, almost every family owned a
television set, one of this medium's functions: knowledge and the promotion
of communication between the nations, became increasingly important. It is
hardly surprising, therefore, that pictures of children in areas of war
(Biafra, South-East-Asia) or in catastrophes went straight to the hearts of
many people (Hoksbergen, 1979, p. 30). The reporters on the spot did their
best to achieve this effect. Speaking in abstract terms, we may conclude
that, from a psychological point of view, the geographical distances between
countries and nations have become much smaller.

Diagram 1: Placed foreign and Dutch adopted children and children born in
Holland, 1970–1986 (1970 = 100)

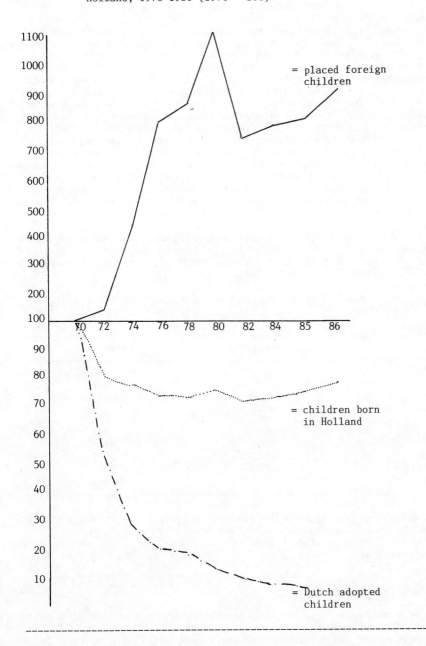

Historically speaking, we think it justified to mark 1967 as the basis year for the adoption of children from distant countries (Asia, South-America and Africa). It was in the very same year that the famous Dutch author Jan de Hartog appeared on television in order to call on people to offer help to the many thousands of foundlings and orphans in South-East-Asia. This was the first time in Holland that someone explicitly suggested adoption as a means of helping these children. The idea not only appealed to involuntarily childless couples, but to couples that already had one or more children, as well. Consequently, from a cultural point of view, adoption became a way of building a family that was within everyone's reach. Naturally, it took a number of years for these effects to become apparent. This process was strongly influenced by the work of various adoption organizations that based their activities on the principle of rendering aid to children in need.

In the second half of the seventies, foreign adoption was frequently and positively covered in the press. This was the time of the Vietnam war and the reports about boat refugees. Adoption organizations such as the Foundation for Intercountry Adoption (F.I.A.), Worldchildren and the Dutch Society for Foster Families had much influence on potential adoptive parents. In this way, many couples were motivated to adopt a child. This is shown by the considerable increase in the number of applications from 1975 onwards.

In the eighties, this situation has drastically changed. Increasing costs and negative publicity have led to a serious drop in the number of applications and, at the same time, to a growing number of cases of withdrawal of applications, except 1986 (table 6.2.).

Table 6.2. The total number of applications for adoption and withdrawals, 1970-1986

year	applications	withdrawals
1970	407	--
1972	1636	419
1974	1312	281
1976	2631	819
1978	2696	404
1980	2897	993
1982	2064	1440
1984	1675	962
1985	1550	1203
1986	1791	565

However, our group falls within the positive period. Costs were not so high yet, and the overall economic situation was very good (practically no unemployment). The media had a positive influence where the decision to adopt was concerned.

6.1. Waiting Period

In the early seventies, couples that were considering adoption of a child generally had three options. They could apply to a Council of Child Welfare or to a bureau for assistance to pregnant women and single parents for a Dutch child. They could try to contact a children's home in a European country or, for the same purpose, apply to the Dutch Society for Foster Families (the adoption efforts of this society that was established in 1950 came to an end in 1983). Finally, parents could apply to the then Foundation for Intercountry Adoption (1969) or the Worldchildren Organization (established in 1971) for the adoption of a non-European child.

In the early seventies, changes within the Dutch adoption world took place in rapid succession (Hoksbergen, 1979, Hoksbergen & Walenkamp, 1983). As a result, adoptive parents sometimes had to adapt themselves if they wanted their desire for children to be fulfilled at all. Initially, they had applied for a Dutch child, but all of a sudden this proved impossible. Then they applied for a European child, but the possibilities in that field changed rapidly, too. From 1970 onwards, however, adoption of children from distant countries became less and less difficult.

The organizations involved more and more often pointed out the difficult living conditions of these children to the couples that had applied for adoption. We said it before and we will say it again, the media were a great help in this respect, too. Between 1970 and 1975, adoption of a child from, for instance, South-Korea, India, Colombia and Thailand, became easier every year. At the same time, however, it presupposed a willingness and capability on the part of the parents to adjust themselves to changed circumstances. Also, that the change from white to brown would have no negative effects on the parents' adaptation to the child and vice versa. In fact, what the latter really comes down to, is that adoptive parenthood, especially when it concerns a first child, is supposed to imply an overall desire for children; where the child comes from, what it looks like, and its sex, are matters of minor importance. There only are outspoken preferences with regard to health and age at the very most: there is a predominant preference for as young a child as possible (although this preference is less predominant when there already are own children in the family). However, when parents are confronted with a particular child via photographs or data at home, or, concretely, in the country of origin, the factors age and health often become less important.

On the basis of our data we have been able to conclude that this willingness to adapt to changed circumstances must have been living among our parents, too. Initially, more than a third of all parents had applied for a Dutch or European child. This implies that from the very beginning the greater part of our group had a non-European child in mind. This is particularly true for the parents that already had own children, or that already had adopted a child.

In 4.3. we already mentioned the fact that in some cases specific preferences were uttered, especially with regard to age, that could not be met (this happened in 25 cases out of a total of 116 (4)). There were only a few objections to this situation. This in itself is proof of the parents' willingness to adapt to changed circumstances.

Did the parents have to be very patient and did they have to wait very long for the arrival of their so desperately wanted child? We know from data of the Child Welfare Council in Amsterdam (Hoksbergen & Van Sijl, 1985) that the waiting period for the family investigation increased rapidly from more than 1 year in 1975 to $2\frac{1}{2}$ years in 1978 and to 3 years or more later on. After the family investigation, many couples had to wait for yet another year (or even more) before the child was placed. However, our group almost completely falls within the more "favourable" period. The waiting period between the application to the Department of Justice and the arrival of the first child from Thailand was not as bad as all that. It lasted about two years. A second child often arrived even more quickly. As a matter of fact, the intermediary organizations tried to promote this practice of adopting a second child, most of all because it was considered better for the first child not to be alone too long. One might conclude from the foregoing, and particularly from the relatively short waiting period, that adoption of a child from Thailand must have been a relatively smooth process for the parents, especially if we compare this with later groups of adoptive parents. What is the parents' opinion on this matter? Of the 116 adoptions, 73 are said to have proceeded relatively smoothly. However, there are quite a lot of complaints about the many organizational matters that had to be attended to in Holland as well as in Thailand. The group that considered the adoption process a rather laborious affair was specifically referring to the long waiting periods.

There is yet another respect in which this group seems reasonably content with the way in which things were handled. We asked them whether, in their own opinion, they had received sufficient information about all the ins and outs of that part of the adoption process that takes place before the child's actual placement. This information was considered sufficient in 88 cases out of 116. If it was considered insufficient, this was specifically with regard to certain procedures one was confronted with in Thailand. Only in four cases had parents wanted to know more about the child. We say "only" because we know from experience that nowadays, parents attach much more value to gathering as much information about the child they will obtain as possible.

From a historical point of view, the afore-mentioned opinions of the Thai group are not so odd. In the seventies, procedures and organizational difficulties took up most of the adoptive parents' time and, indeed, most of the time of the intermediary organizations as well. What is more, in those days one had not as yet gained an awful lot of experience with the children themselves. From the end of the seventies onwards, this situation changed drastically. Nowadays, adoption organizations in Holland consciously try to obtain a considerable amount of information about the child and its past history from the organizations in the countries of origin. This background information is essential for a better understanding of any remarkable behaviour that may be displayed by the child during the first months after arrival, or even during the adolescence phase. This applies to the adoption of older children (olden than 1 year) most of all. Since our group mainly comprises children under 1 at the moment of arrival, the afore-mentioned opinions of the parents about the preparation are no great surprise.

6.2. Guidance

Were there, at the moment of arrival of the children from Thailand, special guidance and aftercare facilities? This in its turn immediately gives rise to the question whether adoptive families come up against other problems than normal families. This is not the place to expand on this discussion. We would rather leave that to the clinical pedagogues and child psychologists. We think that the special way in which the adopted child enters a family (usually a few months or even years old, of another race, often neglected, genetically totally unknown, etc.) poses special problems to the parents and the social workers. As a matter of fact, as a group, adoptive parents cannot be compared with other parents that turn to assistance. On the one hand, there are strong feelings of uncertainty, perhaps even fear of failure, but on the other hand there is an equally strong involvement with the child and the wish to be a good parent. The latter is a result of their strong parenthood motivation, that manifests itself in patience, willingness to adapt, readiness to make financial sacrifices, etc.

However, the question remains as to whether there were special facilities for adoptive families. Unfortunately, the answer to this question has to be negative. Only adoption organizations such as the then Bureau for Inter- country Adoption in The Hague and the Worldchildren Foundation in Amsterdam had some activities that might be labeled as aftercare. Parents could apply for a guest family (after 1976), attend lectures (especially after 1978) or ask the intermediary social worker to visit them in order to talk about pedagogical issues. Assistance, Medical Pedagogical Bureaus, Children's Hospitals, Youth Psychiatrical Services etc. had no special officials for adoptive families to turn to. It is hardly surprising, therefore, that our group of parents mainly answered that there was no special aftercare for them. The aftercare was described as "reasonable" or "good" in only 7 cases out of 116.

In spite of the fact that this group of adoptive parents was not familiar with aftercare facilities, we nevertheless attempted to get to know some opinions about this subject.

This is relevant to the Dutch adoption world right now, because, over the past few years, many attempts have been made to start some degree of aftercare. In 1984, Utrecht University officially started the so-called Adoption Centre in co-operation with adoption organizations and particularly the Faculty of Social Sciences (Appendix C). Rendering assistance to adoptive families forms part of the Adoption Centre's task. In addition, a study group Adoption Aftercare was started (1981), whose main aim is obtaining more knowledge concerning adoption within the existing assistance framework. One hopes to achieve this by appointing so-called attention officials for adoptive families. This has already taken place in 40 of the 60 Regional Institutes for Mental Welfare. The willingness on the part of the existing assistance organizations to pay special attention to adoption problems has increased over the past few years. This development was aided by the special character and growing number of calls for help from adoptive parents (Hoksbergen, 1983).

In so far as our parents make any statements about the advisability of aftercare at all, they mostly refer to it in connection with older or handicapped children. In fact, it is completely absurd that in a country with so many social security provisions and so strong a social engagement, children with a special background should have been placed without any further guidance, for years. This situation did not change until a few years ago, mainly as a result of initiatives on the part of adoption organiza- tions. There now are conversation groups for parents whose child has only just arrived, while parents with serious problems regarding their child's upbringing can partake in special discussion groups (5). That these initia- tives meet a need is shown by reactions from parents (Wereldkinderen, 1984- 3; H. Walenkamp, Maandblad voor Geestelijke Volksgezondheid 5-1984). There still is insufficient guidance for older adopted children. At the time of arrival of the children from Thailand, there were only few, or no aftercare facilities at all.

Important in this respect is the question as to what extent this group of parents has built up certain expectations with regard to their parenthood. Do they expect to be confronted by problems as soon as the child enters the family? These questions deserve serious consideration, because it seems likely that in adoption the risk of educational problems is greater as

parents have built up more explicit expectations with regard to the unknown child. Imperceptibly, these expectations might cause them to "make demands" on the child.

What was the situation like in our group? Eighty % of the parents indicate that they hardly had any preconceived ideas about the way in which the child would influence the family situation. A minority of the parents, however, indicated that they had built up clear-cut expectations. The latter should be seriously considered by the intermediary organizations. It sometimes happens that on the part of adoptive parents that already have children of their own, there are all kinds of preconceived ideas about the adopted child's behaviour. This can be so strong, that a child sometimes seems to have to fit in a particular educational structure, a situation that might have a negative effect on the process of the child's growth into the family.

We also asked the parents to look back on their experience so far, and to see whether in bringing up an adopted child one is confronted by the same things as in raising an own child. Of the 88 parents, 31 indicated that they saw differences. Differences that result from other reactions of the direct surroundings, from the child's background, from experiencing other emotions etc. We consider this outcome rather important and think it should be incorporated into the preparation of candidate adoptive parents.

Do these parents, with reference to the preceding question, expect special problems in their families in the years to come? For 75% of the children no problems are expected. The parents of the other children express concern about both, possible discrimination and problems during puberty.

On the whole, the expectations of this group of parents seem quite positive. In later chapters, we will try and find out whether, on the basis of experiences with the children, this optimism is justified.

6.3. The Need for Contact with other Adoptive Parents

Holland has a gamut of organizations and foundations for special aims or special groups of people. Each Dutchman is a member of one of these clubs. Hence, from a cultural point of view, it will hardly be surprising that there are various adoption organizations- and foundations (6). For practical reasons, adoptive parents are obliged to apply to an adoption organization. Only few people are in a position to bring about a foreign adoption independently. Anyway, the adoption organizations emphasize the importance of a membership of a parents' organization, through which contacts between adoptive parents are promoted. We know from experience that the saying "adoptive parents help adoptive parents best" is no mere slogan. It remains to be seen, however, whether adoptive parents take a similar view and do not discontinue their membership a few years after their child's arrival.

How is this for our group? Taking into account the composition of our group and the way in which the children were placed, a process that required a good deal of self-activity, we expected most couples to have little or no contact with other adoptive parents. This supposition turned out to be incorrect. As much as 56% were still members of an adoption organization (mostly Worldchildren) in spite of the fact that, on an average, $8\frac{1}{2}$ years had gone by since their child had joined them.

To the question as to whether there were contacts with other adoptive parents, only 17 (19%) parents answered no, 44 (50%) replied few, and 27 (31%) replied many. During the interview, many parents indicated that they considered the contacts with other adoptive parents very worthwile and would

not want to miss them. It provided them with the opportunity to get advice
and support on all kinds of practical questions concerning their child's
upbringing.

6.4. The Adoption Status

We know from previous research that parents of foreign adopted children
usually do not find it hard to bring up the subject of its adoption status
with their child (Hoksbergen, 1979). In this particular respect, adoptive
parents of children of another race seem to experience fewer difficulties
than other adoptive parents. In Western society, the necessity to talk about
adoption is something that goes without saying.

> It should be remarked, however, that begetting children by using
> sperm or ovum donors, sometimes denoted as hidden adoption, has
> rekindled the discussion about the necessity of telling this to
> the children. In our opinion, people are entitled to knowledge
> about their genetic background. This sometimes is very necessary,
> if only for medical reasons. We know from the adoption practice
> that the so-called pedigree curiosity is a common characteristic
> for man. How one is to provide children that were begotten in this
> way with this information ("telling") is something that should be
> left to the families themselves. We are of the opinion, though,
> that when an individual has reached maturity, he should automati-
> cally be given the available genetic information. If good informa-
> tion is an essential requirement for adoptive families, the same
> holds true for families that make use of modern reproduction
> techniques.

We asked our group whether they found it hard to talk about adoption. In
only one family the answer to this question was "Yes, sometimes". In all
other families the answer given was to the effect that one did not find it
difficult. Hence, in this respect, the authorities and all other people
involved in the countries of origin (Thailand in our case) can set their
minds at ease.

6.5. The Way in which Adoptive Parents experience their Parenthood

By the end of 1986, more than 16,000 foreign children have been adopted in
Holland. About 1200 children from some twenty countries will be added to
this number yearly. In addition, 16,000 children of Dutch origin were placed
in families with a view to adoption. Each year, moreover, there are some 500
adoptions by a stepparent (legally possible since 1979). We here leave aside
the hidden adoptions briefly referred to in 6.4., and amounting to a few
thousand every year.

What we learn from these figures is that, from a quantitative point of
view, non-genetic or adoptive parenthood has become important in our
society, although, measured by the total number of additions to the family
(about 1% via adoption), it still concerns a small group only.

In a qualitative sense, however, the group compensates for its quantitative limitations through a number of interesting tendencies. First of all,
there is a good deal of contact among the adoptive couples themselves; many
are members of a parents' association. We already saw in 6.3. that this is
the case in the Thai group, too. Due to the fact that everything that has to
do with reproduction and additions to the family forms part of man's basic
circumstances, the group of adoptive parents receives a good deal of

attention from the media. All eyes remain fixed upon them. This strengthens feelings of mutual solidarity.

Secondly, this group is very aware of the responsibilities that their parenthood brings with it. Adoptive parents have to perform quite a few special activities before they are able to obtain a child. This is even more true for the parents of foreign adopted children. As a result, their orientation on and involvement with the child will be considerable. They have been found to go to great lengths to realize this form of parenthood.

It need not be surprising, therefore, that, apart from the media, researchers from various disciplines (sociologists, anthropologists, medical men, pedagogues, psychologists, psychiatrists, lawyers) should pay a good deal of attention to this group, too.

Since the fifties, adoption has become an important subject of research. One of the pioneers in this field is the American sociologist H.D. Kirk. (Kirk 1953, 1964, 1981, 1984). He also was the one that formulated theories about adoptive parenthood. Kirk's theory served as a basis for our investigation, which explains why we focus on it in this section.

On the basis of data gathered from research among about 2000 adoptive couples during the fifties and sixties, Kirk divided the group of adoptive parents in two, according to the way in which they experienced their parenthood. First of all, the group that acknowledges that there is a difference between adoptive parents and other parents where the way in which they experience parenthood is concerned (acknowledgment-of-difference, A.D.), and secondly, the group that does not think this to be the case (rejection-of-difference, R.D.). As far as we know, there has been no replication of this part of Kirk's theory, at least not where foreign adopted children are concerned. What has happened, though, is that the well-known Canadian adoption researchers Christopher Bagley and Loretta Young (1979) have expressed the expectation that in families with foreign adopted children the A.D.-attitude will be predominant. After all, the obvious racial differences make it impossible to keep the fact of adoption a secret. Regarding the Dutch situation, we would like to add that the policy of the adoption organizations seems to be aimed at the promotion of, speaking in Kirk's terms, the A.D.-attitude. The organizations emphasize the fact that in adoption, help to the child in need comes first. Also, that parents should remain aware of the different origin of their child by, for instance, discussing it with the child or by being in the possession of booklets about the country of origin. They also advocate travelling to the country of origin, once the child is older. Because of this policy of the adoption organizations and on the basis of the literature and reports about foreign adoption, our outlook on the way in which the parents experience adoptive parenthood has become different from Kirk's. We would rather speak in terms of internal and external orientation of adoptive parents. In 4.3. we already expanded on this. The R.D.-attitude is more likely among the internally-oriented parents, whereas the A.D.-attitude will be more likely among externally-oriented parents. Within the group of parents with a foreign adopted child as a whole, however, the A.D.-attitude will be predominant, partly for the reasons mentioned before. There is, however, yet another reason for this circumstance, a reason of a more empirical nature.

Earlier research by us (Hoksbergen, 1979) shows that parents do not find it hard to bring up the subject of the adoption status with their children. Our concept of "telling" closely corresponds with Kirk's method of operationalization of the determination of the A.D.-attitude. Our parents will score many points there. Hence, there are various reasons for assuming that Bagley's supposition will apply to Dutch couples, too. We thought it fit to test this by comparing Kirk's results, mainly local adoption, with the results from our investigation (table 6.3.) (8).

Table 6.3. Comparison local adoption (USA) and foreign adoptions (Holland) with regard to the A.D.-attitude. (7)

number of yes-answers	local adoptions (USA)			foreign adoptions (Holland)		
		%	cum		%	cum
0	195	31	–	2	2	–
1	91	14	45	4	5	7
2	117	18	63	14	16	23
3	109	17	80	14	16	39
4	74	12	92	25	29	68
5	42	7	99	11	13	81
6	4	1	100	17	19	100
TOTAL	632	100		87	100	

Explanation: the fewer yes-answers, the lower the A.D.-attitude.

The data from table 6.3. prove the supposition, that among parents of foreign adopted children the A.D.-attitude is predominant, to be correct. It is striking, though, that in Kirk's group the mode lies at 0 yes-answers (does not occur in our investigation), and in our group at 4 yes-answers.

The foregoing might be interesting in itself if it were not rather obvious and, for the time being, hardly more than a description of differences between groups of adoptive parents. Far more important is the question as to whether a particular attitude can bring forth a better understanding of the relation between parent and child. For instance, do parents with an A.D.-attitude communicate more often with their child about its adoption status and is there more empathy on their part where their child's situation is concerned? Does the child trust its parents and do they make it easy for him to talk about how he experiences his adoption status? Or, in I. Boszormeny Nagy's (1973) terms, is there, as a result of this situation, little reason for the child to develop feelings of disloyalty? Having more parents (although the biological parents nearly always are unknown) might cause such a reaction.

   Kirk's investigation proved that there really is a close connection between the attitude of the adoptive parents and the afore-mentioned relational characteristics: communication, empathy and trust. The stronger the A.D.-attitude on the part of the parents, the more communication there was between parents and child on the subject of the latter's adoption status, the more empathy on the part of the parents and the more trust on the part of the child. On the whole, A.D.-parents seem to be ahead of the R.D.-parents from a relational point of view. If this were true, it would mean fewer educational problems in A.D.-families, all other things being equal. The latter cannot be tested for our investigation as yet, but the hypotheses springing from Kirk's theory can. That the A.D.-scores in the Thai group are much higher than in Kirk's group poses no fundamental problem. We expect that the A.D.-parents in our group will have higher scores on the indices empathy, communication and trust.

Before testing these hypotheses we can, starting from our theory about the differences between parents involved in foreign, and those involved in local adoption, expect our parents to have considerably higher scores on all three indices. Is this really so?

The differences really are considerable. For a better comparison between Kirk's data and ours, we categorized the indices in the same way.

Table 6.4. Comparison local adoptions (USA) and foreign adoptions (Holland) with regard to empathy, communications and trust, in percentages

| | Empathy | | Communication | | Trust | |
	USA %	Hol. %	USA %	Hol. %	USA %	Hol. %
low	45	1	48	1	76	21
middle	18	2	46	5	17	26
high	37	97	6	94	7	53

In all three indices the differences are very significant in the predicted direction. It is remarkable that "trust" scores least among American as well as Dutch adoptive parents. We will try to find an explanation for this circumstance in a next analysis.

We now want to test the second part of the theory. We predict that the A.D.-group will have higher scores than the R.D.-group on all indices. Furthermore, we also verify Kirk's findings that "the better the communication between parent and child, the higher the scores on empathy and trust".

Result: there is a positive connection between A.D. on the one hand and empathy and communication of the other. People with a high score on A.D. also score high on empathy and communication ($p < 0.01$). On the "trust" index, the difference is in the predicted direction, but not significant ($p=0.06$). Our data also show, moreover, that a better communication entails more empathy and trust.

In an earlier section, we drew attention to the fact that in Holland adoptive parents of foreign children feel a certain amount of solidarity, and that this is promoted by the adoption organizations. In addition, we also made some remarks about the policy of the organizations. Starting from this line of reasoning, it is to be expected that parents that set great store by contacts with other adoptive parents, as is shown, for instance, by membership of a parents' organization, will have more of an A.D.-attitude than adoptive parents with fewer group contacts. This supposition is well testable for our group.

Our expectation proves to be correct. The more contacts there are with other adoptive parents, the higher the score on A.D. ($P < 0.03$) (10).

We also tried to find out whether the answers to the interview question "Is the subject of the adoption status ever raised with your child?" were consistent with the answers to Kirk's instrument. This proved impossible afterwards, because most of our parents have no problems with "telling", and have done so to a greater or lesser extent. (11).

Given the other afore-mentioned results and significant connections, we think we may conclude that Kirk's instrument is valid for determining differences in the way in which parents experience their adoptive parenthood. Also, that the relation between the quality of the parenthood perception and three important characteristics of the parent-child relation (communication, empathy and trust) is realistic.

6.6. Conclusions

Realizing parenthood through adoption often implies total acceptance of dependance on others. One is often confronted with requirements of which the use is not always particularly clear. Likewise, in fulfilling the task of educator, adoptive parents often come up against all kinds of special requirements that they are not always able to place. This sometimes leads to strong feelings of uncertainty and to a certain need for assistance. For our group of adoptive parents there were hardly any assistance facilities. What we found, though, is that couples kept in touch with each other to a considerable extent and that these contacts were considered very worthwile.

On the basis of the results from the investigation by H.D. Kirk, the investigation that we replied to, it has become clear, for the time being, that parents of a foreign adopted child do not find it difficult to accept their special form of parenthood. The acknowledgment-of-difference attitude is very strong in comparison with the group that was investigated by Kirk. Once again this attitude proved to be important for some important characteristics of the relationship between adoptive parent and adopted child (empathy, communication and trust). As we expected, we found the same connections as Kirk did. The greather the awareness of the special nature of adoptive parenthood on the part of the parents, the easier the communication with the child about its adoption status. In addition, there is greater empathy on their part where their child's perception of its environment is concerned, while the child in its turn, seems to put more trust in its parents. How important a good communication is, is shown, as in Kirk's investigation, by the fact that the higher the parents score on "communication" the higher they score on "trust" as well. Our analysis proves that there is a connection between the A.D.-attitude and the extent to which couples keep in touch with other adoptive couples. It has once again become clear (see Feigelman & Silverman, 1983) how good it is for adoptive parents to be a member of a parents' organization, which makes it easier for them to keep in touch with other adoptive parents. Our data indicate that this often results in a greater willingness on the part of the parents to talk about the child's origins.

THE FAMILY DIMENSION SCALES

7.1. The family as a system

Researchers of Utrecht University have recently developed the Family
Dimension Scales (FDS) (1). The aim of the FDS is gathering information
about the way in which members of the family perceive their family. The FDS
can be used for the benefit of family diagnostics. By having the list filled
in by various members of the family one is able to determine the views on
the family.

We do not aim to use the FDS for therapeutic purposes. We use the FDS as
an instrument of research with the help of which we are able to determine
adoptive parents' perception of their family system. For this reason, the
list was not presented to all members of the family, but to the parents
only.

Which family dimensions are being mapped has already been discussed in
3.3. We will now amplify on the three separate dimension scales (Cohesion,
Adaptation and Social desirability).

The Cohesion scale starts from the "Cohesion" dimension which is defined
as "the commitment that the members of the family feel towards each other".
This dimension consists of five categories:
1. Emotional involvement. The extent to which members of the family feel
   emotionally involved with and loyal to one another.
2. Dependence. The extent to which members of the family need and support
   each other.
3. Coalitions. The way in which the subsystem of the parents and that of the
   children is organized and the extent to which generation boundaries
   between these systems are kept.
4. Boundaries. The extent to which members of the family are oriented
   towards their own family in relation with the external world.
5. Decision-making. The extent to which members of the family turn to each
   other when they have to make choices.

Scores on this dimension scale range from the pole "Loose Sand" (low
cohesion) to "Knot" (high cohesion). In between are the middle levels
"Individually-Oriented" and "Collectively-Oriented".

If the cohesion of a family system is low (Loose Sand), this suggests an
extreme emphasis on individuality within the family, combined with a limited
loyalty to and involvement with each other. If, however, the cohesion of a
family system is very high (Knot), this indicates too strong an identifica-
tion of the members of the family with the family system (over-identifica-
tion), combined with little scope for independent functioning (individua-
tion).

The second dimension "Adaptation" is described as "the ability of a
family system to adapt its powerstructure, role definitions and relation
rules to changes in internal and external circumstances". This dimension
comprises the following categories:
1. Roles. The way in which the members of the family give shape to their

tasks and responsibilities, and the extent to which these are adapted to circumstances.
2. Rules. The way in which house rules are made and controlled within the family and the extent to which they are adapted to circumstances.
3. Leadership. The way in which authority within the family takes shape, punishment rules are applied, and the extent to which they are adapted to circumstances.

This dimension scale consists of the poles "Static" (very low adaptation), and "Chaotic" (very high adaptation). In between are the middle levels "Structured" and "Flexible". When there is too much stability within a family, there is little room for change. If, however, there is too strong an inclination to change, the latter may give rise to uncertainty, because nobody is certain about the rules anymore.

The FDS's last dimension is "Social Desirability". With the help of this scale we are able to find out whether parents are inclined to give a rosy picture of their family. This scale has four levels that range from "very low" to "very high".

7.2. Adoptive Parents Compared with Other Parents

The data of 341 parents of the reference group were compared with data of 112 parents (57 fathers and 55 mothers) of the adoption group (2). This led to the following results on the Cohesion scale:

Table 7.1. Comparison fathers and mothers of reference group- adoption group on the Cohesion scale, in percentages

	Fathers		Mothers	
	ref. group	adoption group	ref. group	adoption group
loose sand	15	5	15	4
individually	35	16	35	22
collectively	35	49	35	43
knot	15	30	15	31

A remarkable outcome of the comparison is the fact that the parents of the adoption group tend to consider their family high-cohesive (collectively-oriented) or very high-cohesive (knot). This outcome does not surprise us. Most adoptive parents consider family life very important. Man and woman consciously opted for it. The decision to raise children often is a joint decision. Their dedication to and involvement with the family is impressive. More than other families, they will want to form a closely-knit whole, and, therefore, members of the family are not likely to show a strong tendency to go their own way. We should not forget, however, that the children in the adoptive families are rather young, whereas there are relatively more families with older children in the reference group (the average age is 14). The older the children become, the more freedom they will be given and the more they will tend to go their own way.

If we compare the adoptive fathers and -mothers, the mothers seem to even more strongly perceive the family as a unity. This is probably due to the position of the mother within the family. In most adoptive families, especially when there are young children, mother is the one that is home most often. Consequently, she will strongly identify with the family system.

We also compared the two groups of parents on the dimension "Adaptation".

Table 7.2. Comparison fathers and mothers of reference group -adoption group on Adaptation, in percentages

| | Fathers | | Mothers | |
	ref. group	adoption group	ref. group	adoption group
rigid	15	24	15	15
structured	35	38	35	55
flexible	35	31	35	21
chaotic	15	7	15	9

Here, too, there is a clear tendency to be distinguished. Adoptive parents more often consider their family low-adaptive or very low-adaptive (structured or rigid). Far smaller is the percentage of adoptive parents that consider their family chaotic. This, too, can be explained. Usually, adoptive parents are parents that go about the business of bringing up children very consciously. They have to, for, long before the arrival of their child, they are asked about how they plan to raise it! Given the long preparation time before the child's arrival and the attention given to the family by their social surroundings adoptive parents have sufficient reason to carefully consider their approach towards their child's upbringing, sometimes, this may lead to ideas about their child's upbringing that are too rigid.

Whether it is pleasant for children to live in a tightly structured family is yet another question. Here, too, we should not forget that the Thai group consists of children that are younger than the children in the reference group. Although the need for structure is different for each child, a clear family pattern usually proves very helpful to young children. This often proves very important for adopted children in particular. Children that have gone through a lot, in a short time, often ask for clarity. They feel secure when they know what is going to take place at what time and what they can and cannot expect. Some children even tend towards a compulsive pattern: everything has to be predictable, the slightest deviation causes them to panic. Our data show that many children find it hard to accept changes within the family (see 9.7.). Gradually the children have to learn to cope with uncertainties and surprises.

A comparison between adoptive fathers -and mothers shows the latter to have a lower score and thus to be less inclined to change. On the other hand, however, more fathers than mothers fall within the category of those that are least disposed to change.

On the Social Desirability scale the comparison between adoptive and reference group parents shows the following picture:

Table 7.3. Comparison fathers and mothers of reference group–adoption group
on the Social Desirability scale, in percentages

| | Fathers | | Mothers | |
	ref. group	adoption group	ref. group	adoption group
very low–low	15	5	15	6
low–middle	35	42	35	25
middle–high	35	40	35	51
high–very high	15	12	15	17

Concerning the socio-pattern on this scale, we may conclude that adoptive parents tend to score higher and hence are inclined to present a rather rose-coloured picture of the (family) reality. This is even more true for the mothers than for the fathers. We had expected this tendency. This tendency springs from attitude and reactions of the social environment. The actions of adoptive parents are followed more critically than those of other parents. We might say that in the case of adoptive parents social control is impressive. In 1.2. we already mentioned the so-called discrimination of upbringing and the adoptive parents' being outlawed with regard to the meddlesomeness of others. However, adoptive parents often find that the "interested" social environment turns a deaf ear to their question or problems. Often, their reaction to problems is: "You started out so enthu-siastically" or, worse: "I told you" or something to that effect. Reactions of this kind eventually prevent adoptive parents from discussing their problems with others. Or, as an adoptive couple described: "In the end, we only answered that everything was going well and we discussed our real problems with people that understood them; unfortunately, not many people fell into that latter category" (3).

We then wanted to find out whether the scores of the adoptive parents on the three scales were interrelated. What we see then is that parents that score high on Cohesion, score low on Adaptation (p < 0.001, for fathers as well as mothers). This means that very closely-knit families are not much inclined to change. When the members of a family are too involved with each other this may lead to a situation in which one is incapable of a critical evaluation of the own family rules or not prepared to do so. When difficul-ties arise in such a family, parents do not know how to deal with them, in spite of their good intentions. Families with a high cohesion score higher on Social Desirability (p < 0.01 for mothers). Self-centered families obviously try harder to make a good impression on the outside world than the less closely-knit families. As a result, they seem to adopt a more vulner-able attitude.

The same goes for parents that are not very willing to change (score high on Adaptation). They score higher on Social Desirability than parents that indicate that they consider change and own initiative important values and do not set great store by the judgement of others.

7.3. Comparison with other Research Variables

We suspect that the family system is influenced by the adoptive parents' having or not having children of their own. For this reason, adoptive parents with adopted children only, were distinguished from adoptive parents that also have children of their own. In the first group, the desire for children will be stronger. Since they are less familiar with the process of bringing up children, however, and probably more uncertain about it, we expect them to look for a rather well-defined family structure to hold on to.

This turns out to be true when we compare the two groups: parents with adopted children only, score higher on Cohesion than parents that also have children of their own (p < 0.05). More than 86% of the mothers without own children score in the highest categories (structured or rigid), whereas only 60% of the mothers with own children do the same. For the fathers these percentages are 82 and 54 respectively. This will partly be influenced by the slightly younger age of the adopted children in the first group.

Apparently, parents that have experience in the field of raising children are capable of giving the members of the family more opportunity for functioning independently, or are more willing to do so. They are slightly more disposed to change for the same reason and therefore have a slightly lower score on the Adaptation scale. They are less afraid of going along with changed circumstances, whereas the group of parents with adopted children only, maintains a more well-defined family structure. The uncertainty of parents without any experience in the field of raising children is also shown by their score on the Social Desirability scale. They score higher on this scale than the parents with experience: in the first group, 14% of the fathers and 20% of the mothers score in the highest category versus 8% and 0% of the parents with experience. On the whole, adoptive parents, and particularly the ones without children of their own, seem, partly under the influence of the social environment, to set great store by making a good impression on others.

If we take a closer look at the development of the placement, we see that families with a well-defined family structure are less inclined to call in the help of others, than families that are more flexible. This does not come as a surprise, for those families that are little disposed to change will not easily contact social workers. After all, contact with a social worker will often involve change. More often than not, these families also are strongly involved with each other and do not easily seek the solution to their problems outside of the family circle. Due to the fact that the numbers are too small, we are not able to find out whether families that are less inclined to change also more often belong to the group with problematic placements, as one would expect them to.

7.4. Connection with the Scores in Kirk's Instrument

The results on Kirk's instrument enable us to gain an insight into certain characteristics of adoptive parents. We want to compare these with the results of the FDS and thereby expect to find some sort of a connection.

We assume that parents with an A.D.-attitude (parents in whose opinion there is difference between adoptive parents and other parents where the attitude towards parenthood is concerned) will score higher on the Adaptation scale and lower on the Cohesion scale. In our opinion, parents that do not hesitate to bring up the subject of the specific aspects of bringing up an adopted child, will be more willing to adapt their family system to this specific upbringing, and hence will have less of a well-defined family system. These parents will be less afraid of allowing their children to be themselves. All these assumptions prove to be true.

We expect that in the families with a flexible structure (high Adaptation), there will be relatively many parents with a strong empathy with regard to their child's perception of its environment. This proves to be true. Parents that are capable of empathy with regard to the situation of their child, also are more capable of reacting similarly towards changing circumstances and of adapting the family system to them ($p < 0.05$). In these families we also expect more Communication. This, however, is only partly true, it goes for the mothers, but not for the fathers. This may have something to do with the role in the family. Generally speaking, mothers talk more often with their children than fathers, and the same might be true for the communication about adoption.

7.5. Summary

The picture presented by adoptive parents of their family system shows adoptive families to be rather closely-knit families. There is a good deal of involvement between parents and children. This once again goes to show that adoptive parents have a strong desire for children and consider family life very important. In addition, adoptive families also prove to be relatively well-structured, which is hardly surprising if one considers the children's young age. On the other hand, however, the disadvantage of this fixed structure is that it makes it less easy to adjust the educational system if this might prove necessary.

   Parents that score high on the A.D.-attitude are more inclined to change, which is indicated by a higher score on the Adaptation scale. Once again, the positive effect on this attitude comes to the fore. The Social Desirability scale shows that adoptive parents tend towards a positive distortion of family reality.

SCHOOL

As we indicated in chapter 3, two instruments were used to gain an impression of the children's functioning at school: the Schoolbehaviourassessment-list (SCHOAL) and a questionnaire composed by us, both of them to be filled in by the teacher. The SCHOAL enables us to gain an insight into the child's socio-emotional behaviour at school, in so far as this is assessed by the teacher. The questionnaire was used in order to gain an impression of the child's cognitive functioning, one of the things it asked for, for instance, were schoolmarks. In the sections 8.1. up to and including 8.3. we will discuss the most important data on these two aspects. In 8.4. we will focus on a group of 7 pupils that eventually ended up in special education.

8.1. Socio-Emotional Behaviour at School

After the family, school is the most important social community for most children. Regarding a child's social development we might say that it is within the family that it acquires its first social skills. It is within this same family that the foundation is laid for the social behaviour that is needed for a good contact with others. It is at school, however, that children are provided with the opportunity to apply the skills acquired within the family, and to expand them, especially where the relation to peers is concerned. The extent to which a child manages to function well from a socio-emotional point of view, depends on many factors. We would like to mention two.

First of all, there is the question as to how far the child has adavanced in its socio-emotional development at the moment of its going to school for the first time. In this respect, adopted children are in a special position. As we have said before, many of them have problematic backgrounds. They were separated from their natural parents and often lived in a children's home for a while, where they were poorly cared for, or even neglected. As a result, there was little opportunity for the development of basic feelings of trust and security. However, children differ in the extent to which their backgrounds are problematic and for this reason we divided our Thai group into two subgroups: the group with and the group "without" a problematic background (see 5.2.). We assume that children with a problematic background are more liable to be behind in socio-emotional development. They will have more difficulty adapting themselves at school and will have a lower score on the Social Contact scale of the SCHOAL than children with a less problematic background.

A second factor that has been known to influence the child's behaviour at school is the level of its cognitive functioning. When a child is less able to meet the requirements of the school, it will adopt a more negative attitude towards everything that has to do with school, for instance the contact with teacher and classmates (Meyer, 1975). In assessing the behaviour at school we therefore will distinguish between children with and children without problems with learning. We expect the latter to have a

- 53 -

lower score on the Social Contact scale and the Attitude towards Work scale than the children without problems with learning. Furthermore, it seems justified to suppose that children with a problematic background will be more liable to have problems with learning and consequently will score lower on the Attitude towards Work scale than children with a background that we consider non-problematic. In 8.1a and 8.1b we will try to find out whether our expectations are confirmed. First, however, we will focus on how, in our opinion, we were able to determine the socio-emotional behaviour at school with the help of the SCHOAL.

The teachers involved filled in the SCHOAL for 102 children, 50 girls and 52 boys. The list was intended for children in kindergarten and in ordinary primary education, so that 7 children that are in special education and 1 child that is in secondary education, fall outside of the scope of this analysis. For various reasons, the SCHOAL was not filled in for all children in kindergarten or in ordinary primary education (1). Of the 102 children for whom the SCHOAL was filled in, 7 are in kindergarten.

Apart from the adopted children, the SCHOAL was also filled in for 2 classmates. The latter, a boy and a girl, were chosen randomly (2). They make up a suitable reference group for our investigation. As a result, we are able to compare the children with the national norm group as well as with the classmates. We decided to incorporate a comparison with classmates into our investigation because the adopted children's schools might not prove to be a random sample of all primary schools in Holland. Exactly because adoptive parents are very child-oriented and, more often than not, are well educated themselves, we may expect them to attach considerable value to a good school for their child. For this reason, a comparison of adopted children with the national norm group only, might present a slightly flattered picture.

The SCHOAL consists of four different factor scales: Frankness, Attitude towards Work, Social Contact and Emotionality. The score on each scale ranges from 1 to 19. A high score on Frankness and Emotionality indicates a great deal of frankness and emotionality. A low score on Attitude towards Work and Social Contact indicates a better attitude towards work and a better social contact. 10 Is the average norm score for every scale. We will give a mere description of the Frankness and Emotionality scales (8.1a and 8.1b).

The scales that are relevant to our suppositions are Attitude towards Work and Social Contact. They provide us with important information about the child's adaptation to school (8.1c and 8.1d).

a. Frankness
A high score on the Frankness scale indicates a great deal of frankness (table 8.1.).

Table 8.1. Average scores on the "Frankness" scale

adopted children	= 9.9	classmates	= 10.4
adopted boys	= 10.1	boys	= 10.1
adopted girls	= 9.6	girls	= 10.7

As a group, the adopted children have an average score of (9.9), versus a slightly higher average score on the part of their classmates (10.4.).

On an average, the adopted girls are slightly less frank than the adopted boys and far less than their female classmates. We see that the proportion between boys and girls among the classmates is just the other way round. Except for this difference, the results on this scale are far from remarkable. We would like to end the description of this scale with the comment that the adoption group experiences no problems in this field at school.

b. Emotionality
This scale describes the emotional aspects of the children's behaviour. A low score indicates that a child reacts very emotionally, is in tears rather quickly, worries about everything and makes a problem out of everything. A high score indicates tough and insensitive behaviour, the "taking care of number one".

Table 8.2. Average scores on the Emotionality scale

adopted children	= 9.9	classmates	= 9.6
adopted boys	= 10.6	boys	= 10.2
adopted girls	= 9.2	girls	= 9.1

As a group, the adopted children obtain an average result, versus a slightly lower score on the part of their classmates who therefore, on an average, are slightly more emotional. Within the adoption group itself, girls score lower and this also goes for their female classmates. In itself, this tendency is not so odd, for, on the whole, girls are more inclined to express their emotions than boys.
There is no obvious connection between the opinion of the teacher (incorporated into the SCHOAL) and that of the parents, where the child's emotional behaviour is concerned. The parents were asked whether they considered their child capable of dealing with emotions in a normal way. Nine parents consider their child behind in this respect, while only 4 out of the 9 children score relatively far above or below the average on the Emotionality scale. To the question as to what parents think of their child's manner of reacting, 9 parents answered that their child is having trouble expressing its emotions and therefore seems superficial. Only 2 of these children are shown to be non-emotional by their scores on the Emotionality scale. Children that are considered to be emotionally inhibited by their parents, do not necessarily have trouble with it at school, that is, according to the teacher. This difference in opinions can partly be explained. For this reason, we should consider the "demands" made by parents on the child's emotional behaviour. Especially adoptive parents are extra keen on establishing a good emotional relationship with their child by doing everything within their power to realize this. It is hardly surprising, therefore, for the parents to expect a certain basic attitude of their child in return. Their criteria, which are based on their own effort, will be higher than those of the teacher, who is less involved with the child. Yet the fact remains that on the whole, the teacher considers adopted children slightly less emotional then their classmates. Perhaps the inter-racial aspect plays a part in this difference. Thailand is called "The land of the smile", where tact and discretion are deemed more important than emotionality.

c. Attitude towards Work

The Attitude towards Work scale focuses on behaviour with regard to learning at school. for instance the ability to concentrate for longer periods of time, rate of work and performance level. A low score on this scale indicates a good attitude towards work, whereas a high score indicates the opposite.

Table 8.3. Average scores on the Attitude towards Work scale

---

adopted children	= 9.0	classmates	= 9.8
adopted boys	= 9.1	boys	= 10.2
adopted girls	= 9.0	girls	= 9.3

As a group, adopted children as well as their classmates have, on an average, a better attitude towards work than the national norm group. The classmates deviate slightly less from the norm group and, by comparison, the classmate boys even have a slightly worse attitude towards work than the norm group boys.

In spite of the fact that, on an average, the total group of adopted children has a good attitude towards work, there nevertheless is an obvious difference within the group itself between children with a good and less good attitude towards work. A child's attitude towards work is influenced by many factors, one of them being performance at school. We are curious to know whether we will be able to also find this connection for our group. For the purpose of this comparison we subdivided the opinion of the teacher on the Attitude towards Work scale in poor, average and good attitude towards work. What we see then is that our supposition is true: there is an obvious relation between a child's attitude towards work and its performance (p < 0.01). Children that are considered bad pupils by the teacher, clearly have a worse attitude towards work than the mediocre or good pupils. A similar connection exists between the occurence of problems with learning or concentration, and the score on the Attitude towards Work scale. Children that have trouble with learning or concentration clearly have a worse attitude towards work (p < 0.01). This supposed connection between behaviour assessment (attitude towards work) and performance assessment corresponds with the validating investigation by Zaal (1978). In this investigation there is a systematic correlation between performance at school and the score on the Attitude towards Work scale.

As we said before, we expect yet another correlation between the attitude towards work and the child's past. A child with a problematic background will have worse school marks and be less motivated to do its utmost at school, and hence have a worse attitude towards work. However, as it turns out, this correlation does not exist and the opposite even seems to be the case. Children with a problematic background have a slightly better score on the Attitude towards Work scale than the children without a problematic past. Children that are in a relatively neglected condition at the moment of arrival do their utmost at school, in spite of the fact that, as we will see in 8.2., they only perform poorly at school. This is an interesting fact that seems to give a scientific basis to the following general hypothesis regarding adopted children: children with a difficult start in live have become aware of the necessity to fend for themselves. These children are go-getters with a strong will to adapt themselves to changed circumstances.

Their vital capacity might prove to be above the average. Where many other children died (Hoksbergen, 1985), they managed to survive.

We do not want to go into our proposition, which might be used to argue in favour of the adoption of "difficult" children. We do think, though, that this proposition might help to explain the good attitude towards work of children with a problematic background.

d. Social Contact
We consider the Social Contact scale very important for our purpose. This closely reflects the child's behaviour at school in the contact with others. If a child comes up against many problems there, this may have serious consequences for its later development.

Table 8.4. Average scores on the Social Contact scale

adopted children	= 8.5		classmates	= 10.1
adopted boys	= 8.4		boys	= 10.3
adopted girls	= 8.6		girls	= 9.8

A low score indicates a good social contact. We see that, on an average, adopted children have a positive social contact. If we compare the average of the adopted children as a group, and for boys and girls separately, with the classmates, then the adopted children turn out to far more positive in their social contact (p < 0.01). The social integration of adopted children even seems to work out better than the integration of the average Dutch child (national norm group). Although this is a fortunate fact, we would like to comment on it. This might well be an example of a case in which the much-discussed positive discrimination of adopted children plays a part. This may induce a teacher to judge an adopted child more positively than its classmates on account of its adoption status. In this context, a comparison with the results of the investigation by Bunjes (1980) is relevant. Part of her investigation deals with adopted children in kindergarten. On the basis of observations of behaviour by nursery school teachers, Bunjes tried to find out whether adopted children differ from Dutch children in their behaviour in class. According to the nursery school teachers, 10% of the adopted children display maladjusted behaviour, whereas this is the case with 15% of the classmates. Bunjes' attitude towards this outcome is sceptical. She observes that nursery school teachers may tend to depict adopted children more favourably than other children. The more so, because her group of adoptive parents indicates that their acquaintances pay extra attention to the child, especially in the beginning.

Is there a relation between the Social Contact skill and a child's past? Is it true that children with a problematic background are difficult to get along with? This is not true. These children even score higher on this scale, just as they did on the Attitude towards Work scale. Here, the same seems to hold true: children that are developmentally retarded at the moment of arrival seem to be doing their utmost to catch up and to adapt themselves to school as well as possible. Apparently, they not only succeed in doing this in the individual sphere (attitude towards work), but are capable of a positive performance in the social contact with their classmates , as well. We might conclude from this that their ambition forms part of an overall lust for life or vital capacity that they seem to possess in abundance.

This outcome contradicts our supposition that children with a problematic background would have more trouble with social contact, but, in itself, it is a positive fact. We should realize, however, that we may not conclude from this Thai investigation that it is generally true that children with a problematic background have a good, or even better potential for development than children with a less problematic past. The problems in the past history of practically all Thai children pale into insignificance in comparison with some children from other countries. Besides, the Thai group is too small to draw far-reaching conclusions. Finally, we are dealing with assessments of the social contact with peers at school. Within the families, things may be completely different.

Let us return to our investigation, therefore, and try to find out whether the teacher's opinion about the child's social behaviour corresponds with the opinion of the parents. We asked the latter whether they think their child is limited in its ability to enter into relationships. Four parents are of the opinion that such is the case. This corresponds with the opinion of the teacher about these children, for none of them had a positive score on the Social Contact scale. Exactly the same picture is presented to us if we ask the parents about their child's relational behaviour towards peers. Four parents answered that they consider this behaviour "different from normal" and these children have a negative score on the Social Contact scale.

Unlike the picture presented to us in the case of the factor emotionality, the opinions of parents and teachers are practically identical. This may be due to the more objective character of this aspect. There is a greater involvement on the part of the parents where the factor emotionality is concerned, and this may influence their opinion.

8.2. School Record

The children's teachers were asked to give a survey of the child's school record in the various subjects. For this purpose they were presented with a questionnaire on which the child's performance could be assessed as poor-satisfactory-good. In this same assessment list teachers were asked to assess the child as a poor-average or good student, in comparison with its classmates, and to see whether the child is having special problems with learning and/or concentration. Contrary to the SCHOAL, the questionnaire was answered for the adopted child only, and not for its classmates. We thought it more advisable to ask the teacher about the child's school record in comparison with the average of the class, than to know the exact marks of two children.

The questionnaire is meant for children in ordinary primary education, hence not for under fives and children in special, or in secondary education. The list was filled in for 94 children (3), 49 girls and 45 boys. We first of all gave a survey of the school record of all 94 children, and then for the boys and girls separately. Girls will probably come out better than boys. In distinguishing between children with or without a problematic background we expect neglected children to perform less well in the cognitive field than children that were not neglected.

Apart from subdividing the group according to background, we also subdivided the group according to the children's age at the moment of arrival (4). We expect children that are younger at the moment of arrival to have a better school record than children that were older when they came to Holland, because they were more stimulated in their cognitive development from a younger age onwards.

Judging by the school records, the children apparently function well. Compared to their classmates, more than 50% of the children perform satisfactorily or well on reading, writing and language. The girls perform better than the boys on almost all subjects. This is a given fact in primary education and it has also been observed among inter-racially adopted children in England (Gill & Jackson, 1983).

Only 2 children have unsatisfactory marks for reading, 6 children have unsatisfactory marks for writing and 5 children underperform on language. We also asked the parents about their child's progress in language. The parents of the children with unsatisfactory marks for language did not have a negative opinion about their child's progress in language. On the other hand, however, some parents of children with satisfactory or good marks for language consider their child behind where progress in language is concerned. Hence, in this respect the opinions of the parents differ from those of the teachers.

Sixteen children have trouble with arithmetic and only a few children perform above average on this subject (this, by the way, is the only subject where boys perform slightly better than girls). This trouble with arithmetic was also observed by the parents when they were asked to give their opinion about their child's progress at school. Many parents indicate that their child dislikes arithmetic and considers it the most difficult subject. As to the rest of the subjects (history, geography, etc.), they all present the same picture: only two children perform poorly or unsatisfactorily, while more than 50% perform more than satisfactorily or well.

When assessing the total level of performance of the child in comparison with its classmates, the teachers assess more than 60% of the children as average, 6% as poor and 30% as good students. It would be interesting to compare these figures with national assessment figures. However, the latter do not exist. So far, we may conclude that as a group, adopted children, on an average, perform satisfactorily in primary school.

Yet, the children's parents view their child's cognitive functioning less positively (table 8.5.).

Table 8.5. The adopted children's cognitive functioning, according to the teacher and according to the parents, in percentages

	opinion teacher	opinion parents
poor student (slightly or considerably behind)	6%	17%
average student (no difference with classmates)	63%	48%
good student (slightly or considerably ahead)	30%	34%

It will be clear that teachers are less likely to take a poor view of an adopted child than the latter's parents. Here, the same question arises as in 8.1.: to what extent might this be ascribed to positive discrimination? Apart from this, this difference in opinion might also have something to do with the fact that parents have higher expectations with regard to their child and therefore will not easily be satisfied with the child's performance. We have already observed this phenomenon at an earlier stage in

connection with the demands made by parents on their child's social behaviour (8.1a). We tried to work out how great this influence of positive
discrimination might be by asking the teacher whether he tends to round the
child's schoolmarks up or down. 71% of the teachers indicated never to round
marks up or down at all. 25% Proved to round marks up and 5% to round marks
down. Since we do not possess reference material with regard to the rounding
up or down of the schoolmarks of classmates, it is difficult to attach much
value to this outcome. It is remarkable, though, that the teachers, in spite
of their positive general opinion, indicate that almost half of the adopted
children have trouble with learning or concentration (5). This goes for boys
as well as for girls. Viewed in this light, the opinion of the parents seems
more realistic. We should add, moreover, that 8 children (8.5%), 7 boys and
1 girl, repeated a class once. It is to be expected that children that are
repeating a class will perform better in comparison with their classmates.
The percentage of children that repeated a class once, is remarkably higher
than the national percentage (2.2%) (6).

8.3. Effects of the Past on Cognitive Functioning

After this description of the most important results of the questionnaire,
we will now go into the correspondence between these data and other research
variables. As we remarked in chapter 3, some questions to the teacher were
also meant to test the validity of other data, such as the results on the
factor scale Attitude towards Work of the SCHOAL. In 8.1c, one or two things
were said about it. Children that are considered poor students and children
with problems in the field of learning and concentration prove to have a
less positive attitude towards work. In this respect, the data of the SCHOAL
correspond with those of the questionnaire.

We also tried to find out whether the opinion of the parents about their
child's performance corresponded with that of the teacher. In spite of the
fact that parents tend to judge their child more harshly, the similarities
were such that both opinions can be considered valid.

What we want to find out now is whether there is a difference in performance between neglected children and children that were not neglected
(according to the age at the moment of arrival). We need such a comparison
in order to be able to judge the integration changes of the various groups
of children into Dutch education. After all, quite a few older children come
to our country.

Children that are older at the moment of arrival prove to perform less
well on all points and to have trouble with learning and concentration
relatively more often than children that are younger at the moment of
arrival (figure 8.1.). Remarkable, too, is the fact that children that are
older at the moment of arrival more often tend to repeat a class (figure
8.2.). Relatively more often, also, do they have to turn to special education (we will expand on this later on).

What we see is that children under six months at the moment of arrival,
have relatively fewer problems with learning or concentration than children
that are between 6 and 12 months of age, or even older, at the moment of
arrival (p < 0.05). This goes for girls even more than for boys. Children
under 6 months and children between 6 and 12 months old differ most in this
respect. When the children are older, this difference becomes hardly more
marked and even grows less. Also, children that are younger at the moment of
arrival turn out to be relatively less likely to repeat a class, although in

Problems with learning
and/or concentration

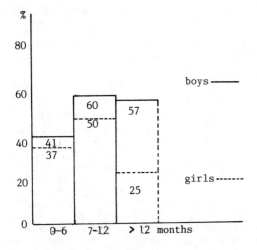

Figure 8.1. Relation age at the moment of arrival and problems
with learning and/or concentration, according to sex

Repeaters

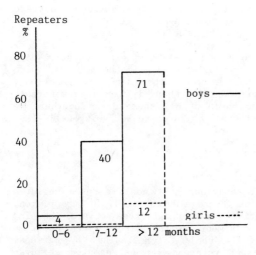

Figure 8.2. Relation age at the moment of arrival and repeating
a class, according to sex

this case, it is the oldest group instead of the middle group, that contains the highest percentage of repeaters.

Hence, the supposition that children that are younger at the moment of arrival are doing better at school, because they were stimulated in their intellectual development from an earlier age onwards, seems justified for our group too.

Summarizing, it may be said that children with a difficult start in life, suffer from its effects later on at school. As· to their cognitive functioning, they seem to have slightly more trouble growing into primary education than children with a less problematic past.

8.4. Seven Children in Special Education

First of all, let us consider the kind of special education these children rely on. Two children go to a school for children with cognitive and educational problems, 2 children go to a school for children with cognitive problems, 1 child goes to a school for children with serious cognitive problems and 1 girl is in the special education department of a school for children that are hard of hearing and suffer from a speech impediment. If we want to know whether this is a high percentage, we will have to compare it with the percentage of children in special education in Holland. According to the data of the Central Statistical Office this percentage is 5.8 for children between 6 and 12 years old. We tried to find out whether there is a relation between age at the moment of arrival and the necessity to turn to special education. Of the 7 children, 2 were under 6 months at the moment of arrival, 6 were between 6 and 12 months old, and 2 were older than 12 months. Compared to the total group of children, these children are "old" at the moment of arrival. What we see, therefore, is that of the total group of children older than 6 months at the moment of arrival, relatively more representatives end up in special education, than of the children that are under 6 months at the moment of arrival. Once again, age at the moment of arrival proves to play an important part in the children's performance at school.

The problems that cause a child to be referred to special education also affect the child's behaviour outside school. According to the parents, these children often are behind in the way in which they deal with emotions. Rather often, moreover, do the parents consider them "different from normal" in their contact with peers. On the basis of all these data together, we consider the placement of only 1 of these 7 children to be "going well" (see chapter 9).

8.5. Summary

With regard to the socio-emotional behaviour at school, adopted children from Thailand are doing better than the average Dutch child. In our opinion, this is largely due to the adoptive parents' attitude towards raising children. The great effort and involvement on the part of the adoptive parents have a positive effect on the child's functioning. By national standards, and in comparison with our reference group, adopted children prove to have a more positive attitude towards work and to be better where social contact is concerned.

The children's school records indicate that their performance in the cognitive field ranges from average to good. They are perfectly able to keep up with their classmates at school, and this is even more true for girls than for boys. The fact that 6% of the children are thrown back on special education can hardly be called remarkable, because a similar percentage of Dutch children is in special education, as well.

The children's background in the country of origin influences their performance at school. This influence, however, is twofold: on the one hand, children with a problematic background have more trouble with learning. This may limit the scope for the development of their abilities. On the other hand, however, these children display more positive social behaviour at school and are more likely to do their best with regard to schoolwork. These two qualities are very important for a good development, even though they do not always result in a magnificent intellectual performance.

The children's age at the moment of arrival in Holland influences their cognitive functioning at school. This, too, is a given fact. More often than not, in the country of origin little is done to stimulate the development of these children. Parents or people that take care of the children pay little attention to things such as playing with a baby, and, once the children are older, there often is little material that might help the child to playfully learn all kinds of concepts. If children are older at the moment of arrival, they often are behind in intellectual development. In spite of the fact that they seem to catch up with their classmates rather quickly, this lag in development still remains noticeable in primary school. To what extent we are dealing with a catching up effect here is hard to say on the basis of this investigation, because too few children are in higher forms yet.

REMARKABLE BEHAVIOUR

9.1. Introduction

Basically, it goes without saying that children that are transferred to another culture totally unexpectedly will have problems of adaptation –over a shorter or longer period of time– depending on all kinds of circumstances. In earlier research (Hoksbergen et al., 1982, Hägglund, 1980), this and the factors that might induce problematic behaviour, were elaborately gone into. On the basis of these data we will formulate some expectations and questions about remarkable behaviour in section 9.2. These questions are of primary importance to adoptive parents, because they will be able to incorporate them into their educational policy.

Because the aim of this study is an evaluation of the adoption of children that have been living here for quite a long time, we will, for chronological reasons, start with a description of the child's initial **problems with adaptation** within the family (9.3.). We know from the litera- ture on this subject (Hoksbergen et al., 1982; Bunjes et al., 1983) that after their coming over to Holland, adopted children often find it hard to cope with the immense change, and react by temporarily displaying all kinds of remarkable behaviour during their daily routine, for instance while eating, washing and/or sleeping. Does this apply to the group of adopted children from Thailand, too, and did their parents find it hard to react adequately if their children showed signs of remarkable behaviour? Are these problems indeed temporary?

We also tried to find out whether among the representatives of our group problems or **remarkable behaviour** cropped up in a later phase (9.4.). We thereby listed the number of cases of remarkable behaviour after the first adaptation phase and the kind of behaviour that was displayed. We also asked the parents whether and where they called in someone to **help** them with possible problems (initial problems of adaptation as well as later problems) (9.5.). The question as to whether and to what extent parents are of the opinion that the problems they encountered had to do with adoption is very important to us (9.6.).

As most of our children from Thailand have been living in Holland for a considerable number of years (86% for more than seven years), we have tried to gain an insight into their development. How often do these children suffer from an **anomalous emotional development** (9.7.) and which aspects of emotional growth are involved? Are there certain **limitations** that narrow down the scope for the development of the child's abilities (9.8.)?

We also presented the parents with a short questionnaire for **specific instances of problematic behaviour** (9.9.), whereby the parents indicate in writing the extent to which their child displays this behaviour. This questionnaire also asked the parents about the degree in which these problems were a burden to them (9.10.). We then tried to find out whether this problematic behaviour might be one of the consequences of past neglect (9.11.).

Finally, we focus on the placements themselves, thereby distinguishing between placements that work out well and placements that require much extra attention and care (9.12.) (1).

9.2. Suppositions, Questions and Expectations

a. Connections with regard to the Child (child variables)

Former research (Hoksbergen & Walenkamp, 1983) shows that the problematic past history of an adopted child often gives rise to (temporary) problems within the family. The following questions therefore are of crucial importance to us: how old is the child at the moment of arrival? To what extent did it suffer from neglect or deprivation in the country of origin, for instance by living in a children's home for a number of years or by being taken care of by different people. We expect to find a connection between a higher age at the moment of arrival and a problematic background on the one hand, and the extent to which problems arise once the child has arrived, on the other.

Another important fact is the children's health at the moment of arrival. Is there any cause for alarm on the part of the parents? Is there sufficient recovery and catching up after possible initial problems? Does the children's health give rise to problems or make it necessary to call in medical aid? We start from the supposition that children that are in poor health when they arrive in Holland will have more problems than children that arrive in excellent health (see 5.3.). Children with a handicap take up a special position. It goes without saying that these children require more care.

A next question is whether the child's sex influences its adaptation. Do the Thai boys (59) display problematic behaviour as often as the Thai girls (57)? We know that there is a slight preference on the part of the parents for the adoption of a girl (see 4.3.). Might this have something to do with they way in which boys and girls adapt themselves?

b. Connections with regard to the Family (family variables)

A question that often arises these days is whether families with adopted children as well as own children come up against problems more often. We suppose this to be the case, partly on the grounds of case-studies and non-representative or disparate groups. However, reliable empirical data are lacking. It is important, therefore, to try and find out whether the group of parents with own children are a high-risk group within the Thai group. Before we can do this, though, it is necessary to see whether both subgroups are comparable where the indications of neglect of the child are concerned.

Another question is whether the number of **adopted** children within a family might have something to do with possible problems. We think that adopted children in one and the same family will offer support and understanding to each other. An adopted child that is alone in a family, no matter whether there are own children or not, might end up in an isolated position. It is to be expected, therefore, that parents of families with one adopted child will make mention of problems more often.

Another aspect of the family structure is the difference in age between the adopted child and the children that are already present in the family. For instance, does a very small difference in age (less than $1\frac{1}{2}$ years) influence the way in which the placement works out? The place in the row of children is something to be considered as well: is the adopted child the oldest child of the family, with younger children coming after (over placement), is the adopted child the middle child (in-between placement) or the youngest or first child? Is there some kind of connection between these

different family situations and the occurrence of possible problems? Over
-and in-between placements as well as an extreme difference in age between
the adopted child and own children are supposed to give rise to problems. On
the basis of these suppositions, guidelines were drawn up for matching and
placement by adoption organizations. It will no doubt be relevant, therefore, to investigate these connections for our Thai group (see 4.1.).

Another general question is whether there is a connection between the
length of time that the children have been with the family and possible
problems. Can it be said that the longer the child has been part of the
family the more problems will disappear? We suppose this to be the case with
initial problems of adaptation: after a period of habituation the child will
end up in smoother waters. On the other hand, however, we expect that the
longer the child has been with the family, the greater the likelihood of
problems in the sphere of upbringing will be, problems as the ones that are
to be expected in every average (non-adoptive) family. In this context, it
is relevant to find out whether more or other problems arise in adoptive
families than in an average Dutch family. Dutch as well as American research
shows that parents of adopted children turn to assistance organizations four
or five times as often as parents of "ordinary" children. Less is known
about the difference in character between the problems.

The history of the family, and particularly important changes (like
moving, divorce etc.) may have repercussions on the child's development. We
suppose that there is a connection between relatively drastic changes (from
the child's point of view) and the occurrence of problems. One should also
keep in mind the fact that every adopted child went through a dramatic
change in its life once, i.e. the transfer to Holland. It is to be expected
that a greater instability after this transfer (many drastic changes) is
likely to give rise to more problems within the family (2). After all, the
child will be less able to draw on the basic feelings of security and trust
and hence much sooner be of its stroke in case off sudden important family
changes.

c. Connections with regard to Adoptive Parents (parent variables)
Often, high hopes on the part of the adoptive parents are considered a risk
factor in the development of problems (Stibane, 1983; Hoksbergen & Loenen,
1985). The long waiting period and the many efforts and frustrations
adoptive parents have to put up with may establish a certain image of the
child. An adopted child that finds itself in such a situation has got much
to live up to and make up for to the parents. High hopes might lead to
disappointments and irritations if the child fails to live up to them. We
suppose that this also holds true for the Thai group.

Sometimes the motives for adoption of a child are divided in two: the
idealistic motives (helping children from the Third World) and the family-
oriented motives (the desire to bring up a child). In 4.3., adoptive parents
distinguished in this way, are denoted as externally-oriented and internally-oriented. It is important to investigate whether motivation for adoption
contributes to the occurrence of problems later on.

Finally, we want to return to the fact, briefly mentioned in 4.3., that
adoptive parents can express preferences with regard to their child's age
and sex. Is it justified to suppose that the more this preference is
complied with, the fewer problems there will be? Whatever the case, we
expect a placement that does not meet the specific preference of the
parents, to work out less well. We should realize, however, that most of the
parents of Thai adopted children whose preferences were not met, indicated
that they did not consider this important (21 out of 25).

9.3. Problems of Adaptation

We asked the parents of the 116 Thai children whether there had been problems of adaptation after the moment of arrival. Sixty-eight children (59%) were said not to have suffered from problems of adaptation.

Of the 48 children that did come up against problems of adaptation, 15 suffered from various kinds of sleepdisorders: not being able to get to sleep, nightmares, waking up at night. Some children had problems with eating, 2; with getting toilet-trained, 1; excessive weeping, 4; extremely passive behaviour, 2; fits of anger or quickly changing moods, 2. A relatively large group displayed a combination of the afore-mentioned behaviour.

We will give some examples. Some parents considered their child very restless at the beginning, aggressive or nervous and frightened. Some children started lying or taking things away. Other children were afraid of noises and nervy, wetted the bed or banged their heads. Very many children did not want to be left alone at the beginning. Some children acted very friendly with everybody, and clambered unto every grown-up's lap.

Often, the remarkable behaviour consisted of a combination of reactions: for instance, excessive weeping and not being able to get to sleep, or a strong fear of separation and problems with eating. Children that were used to sleeping on the ground often did not want to sleep in a bed at first. A few children were terrified of men at first.

There is a close connection between initial problems of adaptation and age at the moment of arrival. Of the 74 children that were between 0 and 6 months old at the moment of arrival, 18 children (24%) suffered from problems of adaptation. Among the children that were older at the moment of arrival, problems of adaptation occurred more often (fig. 9.1.).

Another way of ascertaining neglect is by asking whether the child's living conditions in the country of origin were problematic (3). Our data once again prove that there is a connection between this fact and the extent to which there are problems of adaptation. Children with a problematic background (living in a children's home over a longer period of time, being taken care of by many different people) suffer from problems of adaptation far more often (67%) than children with a less problematic background (27%).

There also is a close connection between the child's health at the moment of arrival and possible problems of adaptation. More than half of the children (12 out of 20) that arrived in poor health suffered from problems of adaptation, versus about one third of those that arrived in good health (fig. 9.2.).

Our expectation that neglect in the country of origin (age at the moment of arrival, problematic background, health at the moment of arrival) is connected with the degree in which there are problems of adaptation, proves to be true.

Did the parents of the Thai children find it hard to cope with these problems? The answers that were given during the interview prove that almost 50% of the parents do not find it hard to deal with the initial problems of their child; the others at first found it hard to react adequately to these problems. This fact argues in favour of a better preparation of the parents for all kinds of problems of adaptation, such as problems with eating, sleeping, contact with others, playing with toys, or very practical things. Something that becomes even more important when the children are older at the moment of arrival. Getting used to the adopted child's behaviour rather quickly and reacting to it in such a way that the difficult behaviour will grow less or even will disappear turns out to be quite a difficult task.

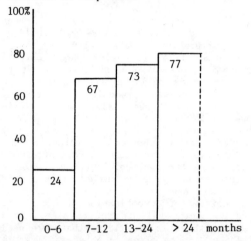

Figure 9.1. Relation age at the moment of arrival and problems of
         adaptation

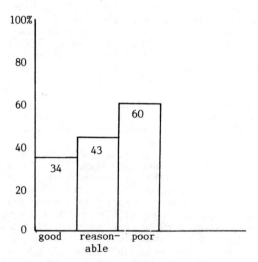

Figure 9.2. Relation health at the moment of arrival and problems
         of adaptation

A question following on from this is whether these initial problems really are only temporary. The parents of 29 of the 48 children (60%) that suffer from problems of adaptation consider these problems temporary. In the case of the other 19 children, however, (40%), these initial problems continued in some form or other. We might conclude from this that temporary problems of adaptation may become the breeding ground of more permanent problematic relations within the family. Whatever the case, we should not underestimate the fleeting character of initial problems. There really are more than enough reasons for proper guidance in the case of initial problems of adaptation, in order to avoid their becoming more permanent problems. Aftercare initiatives on the part of, among others, adoptive parents' organizations, such as guidance of parents immediately after the child's arrival and discussion groups during the first year after the children's arrival are advisable and necessary.

9.4. Remarkable Behaviour after the Early Stages

Did the children start displaying remarkable or special behaviour after their first year in Holland? Of the 116 children 31 (27%) actually did develop remarkable behaviour in the course of time. Among this group are the 19 children whose initial problems of adaptation took on a more permanent character. What kinds of remarkable behaviour are mentioned by the parents? In random order: stuttering, taking things away, aggressive and provoking behaviour, problems with sleeping, difficulty with staying with other people or camping, over-liveliness, fits of anger, problems with learning and concentration, strong fear of death, lying and denying, wetting the bed, feeling inhibited, avoiding conflict situations in every possible way. We will return to a number of specific instances of this behaviour in 9.9.

First of all, remarkable behaviour as it has been described above, is not closely connected with the child's being neglected. There is no close connection between remarkable behaviour in a later phase and the child varibales: age at the moment of arrival, problematic background and health at the moment of arrival. This part of the investigation proved the supposition that children that are adopted at an older age are more likely to display remarkable behaviour, to be wrong. We will ilustrate this with an example. 26% Of the children that came to Holland at a very early age (0 - 6 months) displayed remarkable behaviour at a later stage. For the children that were two years old (or older) at the moment of arrival this is 31%. These differences are very remote from the spectacular differences people sometimes philosophize about. However, for the time being, we will not comment on this fact, because attention will be paid to other aspects of problematic behaviour first.

As for the family variables, there is a close connection between having two or more adopted children on the one hand and a **lesser** degree of displaying remarkable behaviour on the other. Nine of the 19 families with one adopted child (47%) report remarkable behaviour. This goes for only 13 (19%) of the 69 families with two or more adopted children. This might indicate that adopted children can offer understanding and recognition to one another, so that problems are less likely to occur.

It might be useful to try and find out whether in families with adopted children only the likelihood of problematic behaviour is smaller than in families that also contain own children. Do the facts bear out the often heard hypothesis that there are more problems in families that also contain own children? We incorporated this question in our analysis, thereby taking into account the fact that the age at the moment of arrival might distort the picture. The above-mentioned hypothesis is often argued against with the statement that it is not fair to compare families with adopted children only, to families that also contain own children, because in the latter case, the adopted children will often be "older".

Of the 57 families with adopted children only, 10 came up against problems at a later stage (18%). In families with adopted children as well as own children problems after the initial adaptation occur far more often (40%). In all of these families the children were under 1 at the moment of arrival. Because the group of families with own children is rather small (15), we can only conclude that parents with own children do not seem to have fewer problems. Perhaps the view of the intermediate organizations, that people with older own children are more fit to raise an adopted child should be revised. Generally speaking, given the outcome of our investigation, this view seems incorrect. This does not alter the fact, however, that parents with a good deal of experience in the field of bringing up children are very fit to adopt neglected and older children, on the condition that they are better prepared for this task.

In addition, we would like to remark that in case of divorce problematic behaviour occurs rather often (among 3 of the 5 children whose parents were divorced). These numbers are too small to allow for any definitive conclusions.

9.5. Need for Assistance

We asked the parents of the Thai adopted children whether they ever turned to assistance organizations in case of questions or problems. The need for assistance may be indicative of both, number and character of the problems that arose. We would like to remark, though, that we are concerned with the total need for assistance here: for assistance in problems of adaptation as well as in later problems that can either be medical, psychological or educational.

For 25 of the 116 children (until 1-1-1984) the help of an assistance organization was summoned (22%). For 6 of these 25 children, the parents enlisted the help of a regional institute for mental welfare. The parents of 3 children called in a schools advisory service, while the parents of 6 children summoned the aid of other assistance organizations. Ten couples turned to a medical practitioner for help; in their case the problem was mainly medical. If we leave these 10 couples outside of consideration we see that the parents asked for psychological help for 13% of the children. Compared to all Dutch children, this is a relatively large group. Verhulst (1985) mentions 2%, as does Van Engeland (1986). However, these figures cannot be compared, because for one group we determined the need for help over far longer a period (4).

We linked the need for assistance with the various child variables. One of the remarkable things we noticed was that for girls medical assistance was called in more often than for boys. Eight of the 10 medical demands for help were for girls. We also noticed that where the ambulant assistance is concerned, the situation is the other way round: 12 of the 15 educational demands for help were for boys. However, the total number of assistance contacts for boys and girls do not differ much (boys 24%, girls 19%).

When we consider the connection between the degree in which the child was neglected and the need for assistance, we notice the following. The higher the age at the moment of arrival, the greater the need for psycho-social assistance. This is not so odd, for older children are more likely to suffer from problems of adaptation. Moreover, demands for help for younger children often centre upon matters of care and therefore are less often labelled as educational questions by the parents.

An example:

Tim, a baby of 8 months, is anything but a sound sleeper. He cries every night and keeps his parents awake. He has been doing this ever since he arrived in Holland, now six weeks ago. Mother consults with a doctor about these problems and later on turns to a health centre. At the centre, she is given some practical suggestions that may help her to steer Tim's rhythm of sleeping and waking in the right direction.

Neither the mother, nor the doctor would label this **problem of adaptation**, the child probably cries because of the drastic change in climate, care and food, as an **educational problem.** A second example:

Suzie, a girl of $4\frac{1}{2}$ years, has only been in Holland for 2 months, gives her adoptive parents much trouble. Every night, she wakes the other children with her screams. It is impossible to calm her down at night, she seems to be in the grasp of frightful night-mares. Because the parents feel they can get no grip on the girl's fears, they consult other adoptive parents. However, the latter's advice does not work out and after some very exhausting weeks they call the telephone number of the local regional institute for mental welfare. In a discussion with the parents, one then tries to devise a policy that will help solve the problems.

Suzie's problem is similar to Tim's, i.e. problems with sleeping in the habituation phase, but the parents consider it an **educational problem.** Because they do so, they follow a different course than the mother in the first example. They summon the aid of educationalists.

Conclusion: questions about problematic behaviour by children that were older when they came to Holland, often have to do with upbringing. Hardly surprising, therefore, that the parents of these children often turn to regional institutes for mental welfare. Parents of children that were younger when they came to Holland are more likely to turn to medical assistance with their demands for help, because they present their questions as having to do with care rather than with upbringing. General practitioners and (district) nurses therefore should acquaint themselves with everything having to do with children coming from far countries. Some general knowledge about the situation of adopted children, background of adoptive parents, etc. should be gathered. As we know, most adoptive parents consult with their doctor immediately after their child's arrival.

There also is a close connection between the need for assistance and health, the other indication of neglect. The poorer the health, the more often the parents turn to assistance.

For 8 of the 12 children that arrived in poor health a demand for help was formulated. Remarkable and rather unexpected thereby is the fact that in 7 cases a psycho-social assistant was called in and in 1 case a medical assistant. This supports the supposition mentioned before, that a child's age or stage of development often determines whether a problem is labeled as an educational problem. In other words: problems connected with a poor health at the moment of arrival, may be interpreted by the parents as educational problems. However, it is not impossible that a poor health at the moment of arrival might turn out to be the onset of later, more psycho-social problems. This again argues in favour of the fact that doctors or other medical assistants should have an eye for psycho-social problems in the case of demands for help from adoptive parents. Sometimes, the medical assistant will have to know whether to refer parents to adoption experts, a pedagogue, psychologist, and so on.

In our attempts to determine the need for assistance we always have to investigate whether there is a connection between need for assistance and age or length of stay. The longer the child has been in Holland, or the older it is, the greater the chance that help was ever summoned for it. These connections prove to exist in many cases. The longer a child is in Holland, the greater the likelihood of contact(s) with assistance organizations. Likewise, the older the child is at present, the more often help was summoned. Hence, the need for assistance proves to be connected with length of stay within the family and with age. This supports our supposition that questions about older children often enter the assistance circuit as educational problems.

In our group, the need for assistance is connected with a number of family variables. Parents that had own children before the adoption turn to assistance organizations more often than parents with no children, or adopted children only before the adoption (children's age at the moment of arrival being equal). Perhaps, involuntarily childless couples are less willing to turn to others in case of problems. They might have greater fear of failure. Whatever the case, during the preparation, attention should be paid to this fact.

9.6. Does Problematic Behaviour Have Something to Do with Adoption?

Of the 65 couples whose children displayed problematic behaviour at some time or other, 51 think that these problems have **nothing** to do with adoption, whereas 14 couples think **the opposite** is true. If we limit ourselves to these 14 couples, we see that 11 of the 14 families obtained a child that was in poor health at the moment of arrival. Thirteen of the 14 children have a problematic background. Eleven of the 14 children were 1 year, or older at the moment of arrival. We may conclude from this that parents show a strong inclination to relate adoption problems to the consequences of neglect of their child. This was the way in which this question was inter-preted in our investigation.

Originally, the aim of this question was to try and find out whether there was a connection between problematic behaviour on the one hand, and the specific character of the adoption status on the other, **apart from the consequences of neglect.** However, the question, asked in its present form, was interpreted differently. In order to find an answer to the originally intended question, we will have to go into the meaning of the notion adoption status. Possible special pedagogical consequences may not become clear until later (i.e. at a later age).

9.7. Emotional Development

A basic question regarding adoptive parents is whether their children, in spite of both, a difficult start in life and the adoption status, neverthe-less will have a normal emotional development. We asked all parents whether

their child's emotional development is normal or deviant considering:
a. the way in which the child deals with emotions
b. the way in which it reacts, the expression of emotions
c. emotional reactions towards changes
We always asked to compare the child under consideration to its peers. As we said before, it is the subjective perception of the parents we are concerned with. Objective perception, if it were at all possible, is out of the question.

a. Dealing with Emotions
The parents of 5 children are of the opinion that their child handles its emotions better than its peers. For 99 children no difference was noticed. Nine children are reported to show a lag in development and 3 children are even said to show a serious lag. Hence, 90% of the Thai children deal with their emotions in the same way as their peers, or even better. According to the parents, a group of 10% shows a serious lag in development in this respect.
The factors problematic background and age are closely connected with the way in which the child handles its emotions. For example: 3% of the children without a problematic background are deviant in the way in which they handle their emotions, whereas this is the case with 21% of the children with a problematic background. Four percent of the children that were under 6 months at the moment of arrival suffer from this problem versus 31% of the children that were two years or older at the moment of arrival. Hence, a deviant way of handling emotions is closely connected with the extent the extent to which the child suffered from neglect.

b. The Way the Child Reacts when Expressing Emotions
Of the 116 children, 85 (73%) are said by their parents to react normally in the expression of their emotions. Many of them, 31 (27%), are reported to have problems in this field. How do the parents describe these problematic reactions in the expression of emotions? Parents consider their child inhibited rather often, in 12 out of 31 cases. Four other children are reported to react superficially, the children act very friendly with everybody. One child tends to centre its emotions upon one person, two children are whimsical or unpredictable in their reactions. Twelve children are said to display individually deviant reactions: extremely jealous behaviour, a reticence that is very difficult to break through, wild outbursts of anger, intensely emotional behaviour sometimes connected with aggression, quick inflammability with regard to representatives of the other sex, a very negative attitude towards one of the parents. In addition, difficulty in the expression of emotions is closely connected with two of the three indications of neglect: age and health at the moment of arrival. The older the child and the poorer its health at the moment of arrival, the more often it will experience difficulty in the expression of its emotions. There also is a difference in the extent to which problems with the expression of emotions occur among boys and girls. The parents indicate that 10 of the 57 girls (18%) suffer from these problems, versus 21 of the 59 boys (36%). In other words: two thirds of the 31 children with problems in the field of expressing emotions are boys, one third are girls. As we did not expect differences in the reactions of boys and girls, this fact is rather remarkable. However, this outcome can be explained by the fact that twice as many boys than girls were older than six months at the moment of arrival.
We also tried to find out whether time was a factor to be considered in

this question, by incorporating the length of stay within the family and the child's age into our analysis. Children that have been living with a family over a longer period of time are more frequently reported to show deviant reactions in their expressions of emotions. The same goes for age: children that were older at the moment that the investigation took place (between 10 - 15 years old) are more often said to show deviant reactions than younger children. This outcome was to be expected: the more time goes by and the older a child gets, the greater the likelihood of deviant reactions. What is more, an abnormal way of reacting is not recognized and **acknowledged** as such, until the child is much older.

Remarkable, too, is the fact that children that were adopted by more internally oriented parents experienced fewer problems in the expression of their emotions that children adopted by more externally-oriented parents. Perhaps the more internally-oriented parents have a different way of dealing with their child's emotions, which causes them to be more relaxed towards their child's reactions. Because internally-oriented parents often do not have children of their own, they might suffer from the lack of experience in the field of raising children.

When we direct our attention towards the family variables, we notice that problems in the expression of emotions are reported in cases of over -and in-between placements (4 of the 8 children) more often than in the case of under placements (5 of the 32 children). Of the families with adopted children only, 25% have a child with problems in the expression of its emotions versus 50% of the families with own children.

c. Reactions to Changes

How does a child react to changes, such as the transition from home to school, the transition from one class to another, etc.? The parents of 82 children are of the opinion that their child reacts normally to changes (71%). An, in our view, remarkably large group of 34 children (29%) does not react normally. The parents of 19 of them notice growing feelings of uncertainty. Six children are reported to react frightened, which shows itself in not sleeping well at night. The reactions of 5 children are reserved, i.e. they tend to withdraw when a new situation occurs. Two children behave expectantly and display remarkably little initiative. One child even strongly resists changes. Seven children are reported to show individually deviant reactions to change: remarkably imperturbable behaviour (stoïc), bed-wetting, weeping, quickly changing moods.

We did not find a connection between age at the moment of arrival and problematic background on the one hand, and abnormal reactions to changes on the other. Yet, there is a close connection between abnormal reactions to change and health at the moment of arrival. 17% Of the children that arrive in good health are reported to have a deviant way of reacting. The same goes for 32% of the children that arrive in reasonable health, and for 60% of the children that arrive in poor health (fig. 9.3.). At this stage of the investigation it is difficult to come up with an explanation for this obvious relation. Perhaps, abnormal reactions to changes have a physical, vital cause.

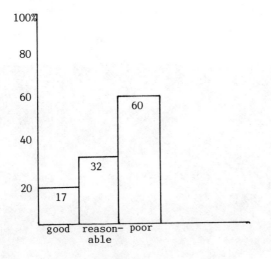

Deviating reaction
to changes

Figure 9.3. Relation health at the moment of arrival and way of
reacting to changes

9.8. Relational Limitations

Does the child suffer from limitations in the field of relations that the
parents consider important enough to mention? What we specifically have in
mind here are limitations caused by physical or mental shortcomings, that,
admittedly, are very different, but nevertheless may inhibit a child in its
social contacts. According to the parents of 107 children (92%) there are no
such limitations in the case of their child. Three children suffer from
relational limitations because of physical shortcomings, and 6 children
suffer from them because of mental shortcomings. These relational limitations are connected with neglect, for they mainly occur among children
with a problematic background or a higher age at the moment of arrival. To
the question as to whether one had obtained sufficient or insufficient
information about adoption (procedure, the child's condition, etc.) parents
of a child with relational limitations often answered that they had been
given insufficient adoption information. In retrospect, it is quite under-
standable that they would have wanted to know more about their child, that
later on turned out to be handicapped in the social sphere. Facts about
background and condition of a child should as much as possible be gathered
and given to the future parents in advance. It is necessary hereby, for the
people in the country of origin, to go about this business truthfully and
carefully and not to make a child's behaviour and health seem better than
they really are. A false impression of things may cause parents to build up
mistaken expectations. This in its turn might cause them to react consider-

ably less adequately to a child's initial problems of adaptation. We now know that many adopted children will come up against problems of adaptation.

9.9. Specific Expressions of Problematic Behaviour

During the interview, we presented all parents with a separate written questionnaire, the "Behaviour list" in which a number of specific expressions of problematic behaviour were mentioned. Parents can indicate on this list whether their child displays or displayed this behaviour and whether they experience(d) this behaviour as a burden. The specific expressions of problematic behaviour are the following:
a. lack of concentration at school
b. superficial relations, "acting very friendly with everybody"
c. hardly shows any real emotions towards other people
d. is inaccessible, one does not get through to him/her
e. not capable of striking up friendships
f. shows no emotional reactions
g. lies and denies
h. takes things away
i. reacts aggressively, whereby one often does not understand the reason for this reaction
This behaviour list draws on data about the consequences of early affective neglect (Rutter, 1979, among others; see 3.6.). The lag in intellectual development, one of the consequences of neglect, often reveals itself in a poor ability to concentrate (item a). The inability to enter into relations, another consequence of neglect, can be found in items b, d and e. The inability to deal with emotions, insensitivity, a well-known consequence of early neglect, has been incorporated in items c and f. A number of specific problems of behaviour, such as stealing, lying and aggressive behaviour (g, h and i), are considered to be consequences of neglect as well. In the next part, we will pay more detailed attention to the various items thereby focusing on the connection with past deprivation.

Lack of Concentration at School
According to the parents, 30 of the 115 children (26%) (5) suffered from lack of concentration at school over a longer or shorter period. We consider this a remarkable outcome for a group of adopted children that were rather young (under 12 months) when they came here. This lack of concentration proves, as was to be expected, to be closely connected with indications of neglect: age and health at the moment of arrival (fig. 9.4.).
Figure 9.4. shows that, in the opinion of the parents, children that were between 6 and 12 months old at the moment of arrival, often come up against problems with concentration later on. This might indicate that being older than six months at the moment of arrival can be a risk factor in some respects.
When we focus on the connection with certain family variables, we notice that lack of concentration is more likely to occur in families that also have own children than in families with adopted children only (ages at the moment of arrival being equal!).
Furthermore, there also is a close connection with all kinds of changes within the family. The larger the number of changes taking place within the family, the greater the likelihood of lack of concentration.

Lack of
concentration

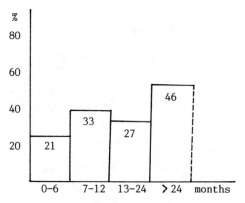

Figure 9.4. Relation age at the moment of arrival and lack of
concentration

Superficial relations, "acting friendly with everybody"
The parents of 12 children (10%) of the total group of 115 children described their child's behaviour in this way. This item proves to be closely
connected with a child's age at the moment of arrival and its having a
problematic background (two of the three indications of neglect).

Hardly shows any genuine emotions with regard to other people
The parents of 4 of the 115 children answered that their child displayed or
displays this behaviour.

Is inaccessible, one does not get through to him/her
The behaviour of 12 children (10%) was described in this way. Inaccessible
behaviour is connected with age at the moment of arrival (table 9.1.). What
was true for lack of concentration is true for inaccessible behaviour as
well: this behaviour is more likely among children that were between 6 and
12 months of age at the moment of arrival.

Table 9.1. The extent to which inaccessible behaviour is displayed by
children of different ages at the moment of arrival, in percentages

age at the moment of arrival	inaccessible behaviour	
	yes	no
0 - 6 months	4	96
7 - 12 months	22	78
13 - 24 months	18	82
older than 24 months	23	77

Inaccessible behaviour occurs more frequently among the older age categories (9-15 years). This may have something to do with ups and downs during the adolescence phase and may be temporary. It is difficult to gain an insight into this situation on the basis of our data only. It is rather remarkable, furthermore, that parents that also have children of their own will consider their adopted child inaccessible more often than other parents. This may give rise to the thought that parents with some experience in the field of raising children perhaps are more likely to make other (higher?) demands on their adopted child and will therefore be more inclined to label their child as inaccessible.

Is unable to strike up friendships
This is indicated for 3 of the 115 children. Although this number is very small the following may be illustrative. Two of these 3 children were 2 years old or even older when they arrived in Holland. Now, the 3 of them are between 10 and 15 years old. Two of the 3 children come from families with one adopted child.

Shows no emotional reactions
Seven of the 115 children are said to display remarkably reserved and non-emotional behaviour in situations where the opposite would be normal. This group obviously is to small to allow us to try and find important explanatory factors. We would like to make the following tentative remarks, though. Six of the 7 children were 6 months or older at the moment of arrival and 3 of them were between 6 and 12 months old. Once again, this young age group seems to carry more risk than one would expect. Five of the 7 children have a problematic background and were in poor health at the moment of arrival. Past neglect seems to have a considerable influence on the children's emotional life, as is shown by various other investigations as well.

Five of the 7 children are growing up in families with own children, while 4 of these 5 children were under 12 months of age at the moment of arrival. Once again, the variable with/without own children seems to call for extra attention.

Lies and denies
The parents of 13 of the 115 children indicate that their child finds it hard to come up with the truth, even if denying is useless. This behaviour is very frequently displayed among children that were older when they arrived in Holland. Remarkable is the connection between lying and denying and the length of the children's stay in Holland. Contrary to what one would expect, this lying behaviour is more frequently displayed by children that have not been in Holland very long yet. Nine of the 13 children with this behaviour (69%) have been living in Holland for a period of between 1 and 8 years, versus only 39% of the total Thai group. This might partly be explained by the character of the problematic behaviour: lying behaviour might be temporary and tied to a particular phase, and be likely to disappear as soon as the child grows older. We notice once again that children from families with own children are more likely to display this behaviour.

Takes things away
For many adoptive parents of children from various countries lying and taking things away are extremely annoying. This was proved in our clinical practice over and over again. It seems to occur rather often, though.

Fourteen of the 115 children of our group were said to take things away and, once again, this behaviour occurs more frequently among children that were older when they arrived in Holland (fig. 9.5.).

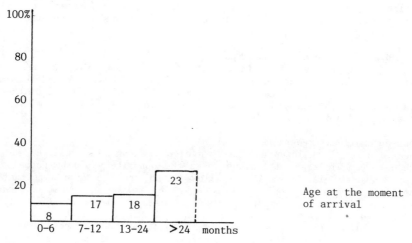

Figure 9.5. Relation age at the moment of arrival and taking things away behaviour

Here, as well as in the case of lying, there is a remarkable connection with the length of stay within the family. Taking things away behaviour is displayed rather often by children that have not been in Holland for a long time yet. We repeat that, as with lying, this may be an instance of problematic behaviour that is tied to a particular phase. What is more, lying and taking things away often go hand in hand and therefore take place in the same period.

Taking things away behaviour occurs more frequently in families with own children. Again, however, the numbers under consideration are too small. Also, this behaviour is closely connected with the stability of a family. This behaviour occurs more often in families that make mention of one or more important changes.

Reacts aggressively, whereby one often does not understand why
Eight of the 115 children are said to display this behaviour. We have not been able to find a connection with neglect. We therefore will have to dispute the usefulness of this item on the Behaviour list.

9.10. How burdensome are these problems for the parents?

It is relevant to try and find out whether the parents experience the afore-mentioned problematic behaviour of their children as very burdensome. If this hardly is the case, this reveals something about the relevance of this problematic behaviour to the general family situation. We therefore made a classification according to the extent to which parents experienced or still experience their child's problematic behaviour as burdensome.

The parents of 37 children came up against one or more of the problems mentioned in the behaviourlist. Of this group, 23 couples (62%) felt little loaded down, 8 felt considerably loaded down and 6 felt very loaded down. The higher the child's age at the moment of arrival, the greather the likelihood of the parents' feeling considerably or very loaded down. This connection seems to be a logical result of the fact that the older the child is at the moment of arrival, the more it will have been neglected and the more often it will display problematic behaviour.

9.11. Effects of Neglect

When we start from the assumption that our Behaviour list registers consequences of neglect, we can try and find out how often the afore-mentioned kinds of problematic behaviour occur. We will also be able to determine which behaviour seems more important judging by the frequence of occurence. In table 9.2., therefore, we have listed the various kinds of problematic behaviour mentioned in our Behaviour list, according to frequence of occurence, thereby distinguishing between children that were under six months at the moment of arrival and children that were older. The latter to once again illustrate the connection with neglect.

Table 9.2. Extent to which problematic behaviour occurs (Behaviour list) among children of various ages at the moment of arrival

problematic behaviour	occurs (n=115)	under 6 mnths at moment of arrival (n=73)	over 6 mnths at moment of arrival (n=42)
lack of concentration	30	21%	36%
takes things away	14	8%	19%
lies and denies	13	6%	21%
superficial relations	12	4%	21%
is inaccessible	12	4%	21%
is aggressive	8	6%	10%
shows no emotions	7	1%	14%
hardly shows emotions	4	3%	5%
is unable to strike up friendships	3	1%	5%

Explanation: 30 of the 115 children show a lack of concentration. Of the 73 children under six months at the moment of arrival, 21% display this behaviour versus 36% of the 42 children older than 6 months at the moment of arrival.

All manifestations of problematic behaviour occur more frequently among children that were older than 6 months at the moment of arrival. This is particularly true for the items lack of concentration, lying and taking things away, acting friendly with everybody and being inaccessable.

It is a pity that we do not have data about a group of Dutch non-adopted and non-neglected children. A comparison might provide us with a better insight into the relevance of the various instances of problematic behaviour. It would also enable us to assess the significance of the results we found. Can the average adoption group be compared to the average Dutch non-adopted group? Do non-neglected adopted children compare favourably with non-adopted children (expectation) in the field of problematic behaviour? How should we assess the problematic behaviour of children that have been neglected when we compare them with non-adopted children? We will have to incorporate these questions into our investigation at a later stage.

9.12. **Assessing the Placement**

Four judges assessed the, anonymous, written data of the interview. In this way, an opinion was obtained on the development of the adoption placement. In the opinion of the judges, the placement in 19 families (16%) called for extra care and attention. There is a close connection between the assessment of the placement and two indications of neglect: age at the moment of arrival and problematic background (fig. 9.6.).

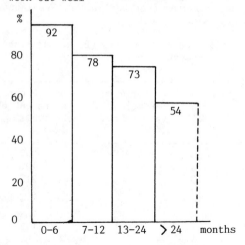

Figure 9.6. Relation age at the moment of placement and assessment of the placement

Although the total group comprises equal numbers of boys and girls, this is different for the group of "problematic placements" where 14 of the 19 children are boys. Here, however, we should repeat our earlier warning that there are twice as many boys as girls among the children that were over six months of age at the moment of arrival. As for problematic background: here the proportion is the same. Given these differences between boys and girls, the problematic development of the placement of boys in adoptive families is predictable and allows of no conclusion to the effect that that the development in the case of boys should be more problematic just because they are boys.

9.13. Conclusions

a. Problems of adaptation are very important
More than 40% of the children suffer from remarkable problems of adaptation, which is a considerable number if one takes into account that these children came to Holland at a comparatively young age. We also might conclude that among children that come to Holland at a relatively later age problems of adaptation will occur more often and will be more serious. In our group, too, there is a close connection between age at the moment of arrival and occurence of problems of adaptation. Remarkable is the fact that in some respects the group of children between 6 and 12 months old at the moment of arrival can be considered a risk group, too. Yarrow and his associates found also that infants separated after 6-7 months of age showed evidence of socio-emotional maladjustment. (Yarrow, 1965; Yarrow and Goodwin, 1973.)

Because a large number of the parents find it hard to react adequately to the problems of adaptation, special attention should be given to this aspect in the preparation. The more so, because there are indications that temporary problems of adaptation may well take on a more permanent character.

b. Effects of neglect deserve a good deal of attention
Neglect described as: older than six months at the moment of arrival, problematic background and poor health at the moment of arrival, gives a less favourable prognosis for the development of the child's emotional and social growth. It is most of all a decisive factor in the development of all kinds of problems of adaptation. There also is an obvious relation with later problems, although here, family situation and family structure are important factors as well.

Neglected children prove to have great difficulty in dealing with emotions in a normal way and with displaying the correct emotional behaviour in situations where this is expected of them. Quite a few children are reported to be very inaccessible or to react non-emotionally.

Our Behaviour list seems a reasonably effective means of measuring neglect. The item "lack of concentration" is mentioned most. Two other possible effects of neglect: lying and taking things away behaviour seem to be tied to a particular phase and therefore to be temporary. All items on the Behaviour list occur more frequently among children that were over six months of age at the moment of arrival.

c. The adoptive family
Repeatedly, certain problems of adaptation occur more frequently in families with own children (ages at the moment of arrival being equal). These parents also seem to be less able to take a lot. Whatever the case, they experience the problems as more burdensome than other parents. In future research, we will try and analyse this.

Involuntarily childless couples seem to find it harder to turn to official assistance organizations in case of problems.

A certain instability within the family seems to have a negative effect on the children. More frequently mention is made of deviant emotional behaviour on their part and of a greater need for help on the part of the parents. On the whole, there seems to be a relatively great need for guidance among adoptive families.

ATTACHMENT IN THE ADOPTIVE FAMILY

10.1. Introduction

For adoptive parents the development of relationships within the family is
fundamentally important, relations between adoptive parents and adopted
child, as well as between the adopted child and the other children in the
family. Essential in this respect is whether, after a number of years, one
can speak of attachment between parents and adopted child or of a familial
bond between the children.

In 10.2. we will fit the notion of "attachment" in a theoretical framework and go into it briefly, thereby focusing on the effects of neglect of
the child on its attachment to the adoptive parents and on the extent to
which it feels at ease with possible other children. We will then formulate
some expectations and questions concerning the development of relations
within the family. In discussing the results of the investigation we will
first of all focus on the bond between parents and child (10.4. and 10.5.).
Do the parents consider the relationship with the child satisfactory
(whereby we investigate this for father and mother separately)? Do they
consider the bond strong or superficial? Does the relationship require much
effort on their part? Important in this respect is whether the bond between
both parents and the adopted child came about easily or with difficulty
(10.6.). Apart from the relationship between parent and child we also pay
attention to the ties between the adopted child and its brothers and sisters
(10.7.). Finally, in 10.8. we will return to the central question whether
the development of relationships in families with Thai children proceeds
well.

Last but not least, in determining the relationships within the family we
started with the opinions and attitudes of the parents. We consider the
subjective perception of the parents, i.e. how they experience and perceive
the relations within the family, very important for a first investigation
into the attachment of older children in adoptive families. This investigation does not deal with objective approaches towards the relations - if
this were at all possible.

However, we attempted to develop an instrument that would allow us
to gain an insight into the process of attachment within the
adoptive families. In reports that will be published later on we
will go into the way in which we made the notion of attachment
operational, and will pay attention to the analysis of the adapted
instrument of Thomas and Chess and its comparison with aspects of
attachment to be discussed in the following sections.

10.2. Attachment and Adoption

Attachment is generally defined as a lasting affective relationship between
a person and a specific other person (Riksen-Walraven, 1983). An attachment
relationship develops between practically every child and its most important
care-taker and is mainly established at the end of the first year of the

child's life. Bowlby's theories, that formed the basis for attachment research, indicate what is meant by a "good" attachment relationship. Generally speaking, one might say that a child is well attached to its parents, often indicated as "securely" attached, if there is a balance between the following tendencies. The child seeks the proximity of the one it is attached to, while exploring and discovering the world. The balance is disturbed when the child is continually seeking proximity by clinging to the care-taker. This balance is disturbed, too, when the child only plays, explores and discovers without needing its parents. In both cases the attachment is insecure, rather than secure.

Remarkable is the fact that in Bowlby's opinion the quality of the attachment relationship between a baby of 12 months and its educator is a decisive factor where its later development is concerned. Research shows that a secure attachment relationship has positive consequences for, among others, co-operating with and obeying the parents, contact with peers and competence in the cognitive field.

One of the pressure points in current attachment research is that the bond between parent and child is difficult to determine. There is a generally accepted way of determining the attachment between a baby of 12 months and its care-taker - via the so-called Strange Situation Procedure (Ainsworth, 1978) - but for the period afterwards no such instruments exist.

It is generally assumed that the development of attachment during the first year of the child's life passes through various stages (Van IJzendoorn, 1979; 1982). In the first 6 months the child gradually starts making out people, but still has little preference for a care-taker. From the age of 6 months onwards, a baby more and more starts to distinguish between people: smiling to acquintances and refusing to do so to strangers, etc. Well-known is the shyness one often observes in that period: the baby turns away from strangers and shows a strong preference for the person it is beginning to get attached to. Towards the end of the first year there is a clearly visible attachment between mother and/or father and child. In the meantime the baby has come to understand that a short separation from the person it has become attached to, is not dramatic. It has formed an internal picture of this person that continues to exist, even if the person in question is absent for a while. The baby is able to bridge a separation, because it knows that mother will return time and again. So far a short description of how attachments normally develop.

It will be clear that in adoption attachment is more complicated. Not only does the relationship between parent and child start at a later time than birth, but the past histories of parents and child are remarkable as well. Often, the child has been living in a children's home or at various addresses for some time and has not been in a position to develop a secure attachment relation- or the rudiments of it. What is more, it has gone through at least one dramatic separation experience when it was forced to take leave of its care-takers in the country of origin. The said period of deprivation and separation experiences can have a negative influence on the quality of the child's potential for attachments (Yarrow, 1965). On the other hand, however, it often happens that adoptive parents are not prepared for parenthood of emotionally neglected children (Hoksbergen and Loenen, 1985). Dealing with a deprived child certainly requires specific abilities, such as much effort on the part of the parents as well as attention so as to be able to assess the child's essential needs.

As to the future relationship between parents and adopted child, here the picture is not entirely optimistic. Up till now, all research has shown that the bulk of the adoptions work out well and that a satisfactory bond is established between parents and child (Van Buuren, 1983). However, there are adoptions that work out less well or even become problematic. There where difficulties arise we often come upon complaints in the social sphere: in developling relationships with parents, brothers or sisters and with peers.

In our Thai investigation we first of all want to provide a basis for further research into attachment in adoptive families by asking a number of general questions about the child's ability to develop relationships. With the help of the answers to the parents' list we will try to come to a more specific definition of the relation between parent and child. This question-naire will be worked out in detail at a later phase.

10.3. Questions and Expectations

A general conclusion that can be drawn from previous attachment research is that children from children's homes will in the long run display a different pattern of attachment (Rutter, 1979). Sometimes, these children desperately cling to one or more adults, or are incapable of entering into profound relations (insensitivity), or they tend to act too friendly with strangers (see 9.7.). Other children act on the defensive. They are averse to much attention and particularly to hugging and kissing or other physical ap-proaches.

Before they came to Holland, adopted children from Thailand spent longer or shorter periods of time in children's homes or were taken care of by different people. It is to be expected, therefore, that children that come to Holland at the age of six months or older, will find it harder to develop a profound relationship with their parents. As it is generally assumed that a child starts getting attached to its care-taker in the second half of the first year of its life, we again distinguish between children that were under six months of age when they came to Holland and children that were older. We suppose that the first group will stand the best chance of developing a normal attachment relationship with the adoptive family. This does not mean to say, however, that we expect all children that were older than six months to have or develop lasting relational problems. We hope and expect that the effects of deprivation can be undone, either partly or completely. Our clinical experiences point in that direction.

Apart from this question we also are curious to know whether the expec-tations cherished by the parents before the child's arrival, played a part in the development of a relationship. In addition, we will also try to find out whether the first meeting with the child and the parents' first impres-sions on that occasion, influenced their subsequent relationship with the child.

10.4. Relationship between Mother and Child

The mothers of 110 of the 115 (1) Thai children (96%) consider the relation-ship with their child satisfactory or very satisfactory. In 3 cases did they consider the relationship reasonable and in 2 cases unsatisfactory. If the supposition uttered in 10.3., would be correct, we might expect these 5 children to be older than six months at the moment of arrival. This is not so. Two children were younger than six months. However, here too, testing is impossible because in this respect there is too little differentiation within the group (and thank goodness this should be so).

The bulk of the relationships between mother and Thai children are said to be satisfactory, which is a very positive result. According to the parents, the bond that develops between mother and child is good in most cases, even if the child has suffered from severe neglect.

We also asked the mothers whether they considered the bond with the child strong enough, 98% answered in the affirmative; the bond between mother and child was said to be superficial in 2 cases only. Remarkable, though, is the fact that these children were older than six months at the moment of arrival. The overall picture, however, shows the development of a strong bond between mother and child in almost all Thai adoptions. The most important manifestations of the child's attachment to its mother are: hugging and kissing (22%), seeking the mother's attention (25%) or a combination of both (35%) (2).

We also asked the mothers whether the relationship requires much effort on their part. 81% Indicated that this was not so. Much or a varying amount of effort was required of the other mothers, whereby there is no difference between children younger or older than six months at the moment of arrival!

Remarkable, furthermore, is the fact that there is a connection between mother's reaction during her first meeting with the child and her dedication to the relationship later on (3). If mixed or negative feelings formed part of mother's first impression of the child, it will often happen that much effort is required of her later on. We suspect that this closely reflects the subjective perception of a relationship. If mother and child do not hit it off from the first moment onwards, mother can lastingly keep the feeling that much is required of her. If, however, the first reaction is positive, a mother will tend to consider her effort (even if it is considerable) normal.

10.5. Relationship between Father and Child

Most fathers (96%) consider their relationship with the child (very) satisfactory. This outcome is similar to that of the relationship between mother and child. Three of the 4 children whose fathers are less content about the bond with their child were older than six months at the moment of arrival. Once again, the numbers are too small to allow real testing.

Most bonds between father and child (97%) are said to be sufficiently strong. Only 3 father-child relationships are said to be superficial. As with the mothers, this concerns children that were older than six months at the moment of arrival. 19% Of the children show their attachment to their father by hugging and kissing, 28% seek the father's attention, and 27% of the children display a combination of this behaviour (4).

89% Of the fathers indicate that the relationship does not require much effort on their part. In comparison with the relationship between mother and child, the relationship between father and child is less likely to require much effort of the father. This outcome is not so odd if one realizes that mother accounts for most of the daily upbringing.

As with the mothers, there is a connection between father's feelings at the first meeting with the child and his later effort. In case of mixed or negative feelings, fathers are more likely to consider the effort required of them later on rather great (3).

10.6. Did the Relationship Come about Easily?

We asked the parents whether the relationship between the adopted child and themselves came about easily or with difficulty. This is important, especially for the future generation of adoptive parents. It is useful to know whether one should prepare for an uncomplicated or difficult start when establishing a bond with the child.

In the case of 102 of the 116 children (88%) the relationship between both parents and the adopted child came about easily and as a matter of course. In 8 cases (7%) did the relationship come about with some difficulty, or is still in process of development. If we take the ages at the moment of arrival into consideration, we notice a remarkable difference. Only for 3 (4%) of the 74 children under six months of age at the moment of arrival, did the relationship come about with (some) difficulty, versus 11 of the 42 children that were older at the moment of arrival.

10.7. Relationship with the other Children in the Family

What is the relationship between the Thai adopted child and the other children within the family like? To 7 children this question does not apply because they are an only child. For 104 (95%) of the other children, the relationship with brothers or sisters - adopted or own - is normal. Only 5 children are said to have a relationship with other children in the family that is "different from normal". This outcome is very favourable; generally speaking, the Thai children's growing into the bunch of children does not give rise to problems. Due to the small numbers we are dealing with, further analyses are impossible, for instance distinguishing between families with and without own children.

10.8. Conclusions

The feelings experienced by father as well as mother during the first meeting with their adopted child often influence the way in which they perceive the effort that the subsequent relationship requires of them. In case of mixed or negative feelings, they feel that the development of the bond requires much effort on their part. Yet, there is no connection between experiencing these feelings and a less close or less satisfactory relationship. Even those parents that consider the relationship satisfactory feel that the effort required of them is above the average. We suspect, therefore, that the "effort" experienced by the parents has got something to do with their subjective perception of the relationship.

Children older than six months at the moment of arrival stand a greater chance of a difficult start of the relationship between parents and child than children that were younger at the moment of arrival. However, in the bulk of the families the parent-child relationship develops as a matter of course.

In most of the families with Thai adopted children, the mother-child and father-child relationships seem satisfactory and strong. The relationships between adopted and own children seem normal.

Developing relationships within a family does not seem to pose serious problems to Thai children and does not seem to be influenced by the negative effects of neglect. This may indicate that:
a. The effects of deprivation can largely be undone, at least in the social sphere;
b. there may be protective factors in the adoption situation that reduce the risks of deprivation and separation experiences (Garmezy & Rutter, 1983). The afore-mentioned "surplus" on the part of the parents and the fact

that these children are desired very much might be examples of such factors. Likewise, there might be protective factors on the part of the children themselves, such as temperament or will to survive.

In the few cases that the development of relationships proves problematic these problems are immense. One child was removed from the parental home for a considerable period of time, while the behavioural disturbances that some other children suffered from, had a negative influence on the parent-child relationship. If problems arise, therefore, it often proves rather difficult to solve them. However, let us repeat that only a limited number of children older than six months at the moment of arrival develop really serious relational problems.

THE INTEGRATION OF THAI CHILDREN
IN THE DUTCH COMMUNITY

11.1. Considerations for the People Involved in the Country of Origin

Adoption of children should be approached with the utmost of care. The interests of child, adoptive and natural parents are immense. In this respect there is not much difference between local and intercountry adoption. The only thing that could be remarked with regard to intercountry adoption is that there adoption seems to be an even greater radical change. After all, the child is transferred over a considerable distance to a country with a different culture and with people of a different race.

This necessary carefulness, however, should not be at the expense of the child's future prospects and chances of development. Our investigation once again shows how harmful it is for children to have to do without basic life conditions such as security, care, attention, stimulation and love for some time. Neglect of children has a negative influence on various abilities of the child and causes the parents to rack their brains over the best way of bringing up their child. All of this indicates that, if children are considered adoptable according to the rules and customs of a country, one should go about this business as soon as possible.

Prolonging the child's sorry existence with a few months or sometimes even a year or more because of some supposedly necessary procedures, has a very negative effect on the same child. In every country, therefore, one should critically investigate the adoption procedure and the time everything takes. In our opinion, one of the ways of shortening procedures is by only working with officially recognized organizations that should be inspected regularly. Acquiring a certain degree of routine and efficiency in this complicated work might save a lot of time.

However, this is not the place to enlarge on all kinds of intricate procedures. We are more interested in the pedagogical effects.

There is a second aspect that calls for our attention. Adopted children always have a specific past history. Even if they are adopted a few weeks after their birth, their genealogical tree nevertheless differs from that of their adoptive parents. Knowledge of important details concerning the original parents and family could be available to the child in future and the parents at once. Often, however, little or nothing will be known about the natural environment, especially when the child was abandoned. However, something may be known about the child's history from the moment of its birth onwards. For many reasons, it is very important that adoptive parents should know as much as possible about the child's background. The preparation of the parents and the prospects of the child will benefit from it. Hence, it is fundamentally wrong to withhold important data. Sometimes, people are under the impression that they serve the adoptive parents well by doing this, because the things that should be told are far from nice. This is not so. Likewise, keeping people in the dark about the correct age of their child is extremely harmful. If one has not got anything to offer but an estimate of the child's age one should say so.

Where adoptive parents benefit from openness and completeness of data from the child's arrival onwards, the child benefits from it later on. As soon as children approach adolescence, they become increasingly dubious about their background and feel the need to attain a clear indentity. This goes for all adolescents, but for adopted children in particular. In their case, some facts are bound to remain unknown. The way in which the adopted children will exhibit these identity problems differs from person to person. What is clear, though, is that knowledge about their background is important to them. It sometimes happens that the people involved dispose of important factual material that might have been useful to the adoptive parents.

In this respect, we want to urge the necessity of the greatest possible carefulness and openness.

11.2. Consequences for the Adoption Organizations in Holland

Our investigation, and the data gathered from previous research show that adoption of foreign children is a rather tricky business. Over the past few years, a good deal of attention has been paid to the procedure used by the organizations involved. Many have urged the necessity of setting high qualitative standards where the matching of the parents and the eventual placement of the child are concerned. That extra attention should be paid to for- and aftercare has already been discussed.

Everyone of us agrees that the preparation of adoptive parents in Holland should be improved. Our data indicate that a poor preparation of the parents results in a more problematic development of the adoption. Well-prepared parents seem more able to cope with possible problems in the child's upbringing. Adopting Holland and the authorities concerned should take the improvement of the preparation of the parents to heart. Organizing a meeting of parents on a voluntary basis once or twice, as is the current practice, is not enough. Much as we value the good works performed by various volunteers all over Holland, the preparation should receive far more attention. The knowledge is available, informative pictures were created and sufficient relevant literature is at hand. What is missing has to do with accepting a new view on the family investigation and the close connection between the latter and the general preparation of the candidate adoptive parents. What has also been lacking so far, is a readiness to make temporary investments, thereby starting from the idea that preventing problems with upbringing will diminish the necessity of appealing to an assistance organization later on and will thus cause a reduction in costs.

Over the past few years, much attention has been paid to aftercare. In this respect, the tide is gradually taking a turn for the better. The Department of Justice even subsidized the Intercountry Adoption Foundation for a number of years. In Holland we thereby are in the fortunate position that at one of our universities a centre for investigation and assistance developed for adoptive parents and adopted children (appendix C). In this way, a certain continuity in the knowledge about the special problems in adoptive families is guaranteed. This knowledge should first of all be passed on to workers of all kinds of adoption organizations involved and to institutions for (mental) welfare throughout the country. Whatever the case, adoptive parents and adopted children can now turn to experts in the field of adoption with, sometimes, very specific questions and problems.

Improvement in for- and aftercare implies, though, that all adoption organizations, ± 10 in Holland, should co-operate to some extent. This means, working at the same qualitative level, dividing tasks, providing general information about the children's situation. In addition, they should also provide the parents with similar suggestions for preparation (we almost said with the same requirements in the field of preparation) and with information about possibilities in the field of guidance and aftercare when the child has arrived. A harmonious co-operation between organizations that are considered bona fide by an impartial third party (Department of Justice) and that do not try to outdo each other here or in other parts of the world, is a conditio sine qua non for creating such a situation. Adoptive parents and adopted children will benefit from it.

11.3. Experiences in 88 Adoptive Families with 116 Children from Thailand, Summary of the most Important Data

Children from Asia adapt themselves well in Dutch families. This obviously is not true for all adopted children but we cannot but conclude from our experiences with the 116 children from Thailand, that the integration in our community is going well. That is to say, for children that have not entered the second exploration phase (the first is the period between 1 and 3 years) i.e. puberty, yet. In spite of these positive conclusions, however, some fundamental comments should be made. Or, in other words, we should like to strike a warning note.

First of all, more often than not the children's medical situation, even though they sometimes were very young when they arrived here, was poor or even bad. In this respect, parents should always be extremely careful. A thorough physical examination with attention for teeth, nose, ears, vitamin situation and skin and intestinal parasites, should take place immediately on arrival. A few years ago, excellent schemes were developed for this purpose, partly on the initiative of the paediatricians Polman, Sorgedrager and Schulpen (1). Medics with ample experience in the field of all kinds of medical specialities such as tropical diseases among foreign adopted children that are practically unknown in the West. Some tropical diseases only occur in certain specific areas which makes this an uncertain factor.

On the other hand, however, the children prove to always recover well from a medical point of view. Effects of malnutrition, all kinds of diseases and parasites, can be undone. In our opinion, this could indicate that the children are above the average where vitality and willpower are concerned.

A second consideration, that concerns all adoptive parents, is the perception of parenthood. There are differences between natural and adoptive parenthood that cannot be disregarded. Parents of interracially adopted children seem more aware of this fact than other adoptive parents. Needless to say, this is promoted by the clearly visible difference in race between parents and child. The importance of the acknowledgment-of-difference attitude has come to the fore in this group that, as a whole, possesses this attitude in a considerable degree. What goes for the adoptive parents in Kirk's American investigation, goes for our parents as well, namely that the more parents are aware of the special character of adoptive parenthood, the easier it is for them to talk with their child about its adoption status.

In addition, there is more empathy on their part with regard to the way in which their adopted child perceives its environment, with the subsequent result that the child puts more trust in its parents. Adoptive parents should be open to their child about its adoption status. All our research and clinical experiences point in that direction. There are matters, moreover, that stimulate this openness. In this context, we would advise the parents to keep in touch with other adoptive parents, for instance through a membership of a parents' organization. Many parents already do this, which to us is proof of the adoptive parents' intense involvement with the ups and downs of their children. Adoptive families are closely-knit families. The wish to associate with children and to raise them and the importance that is attached to family life are considerable. The rigorously structured character of many of these families, however, may entail the danger of there being too little willingness to change. The latter happens to be essential in the adoption of older children, that often have a problematic background.

This brings us to a third area to be considered: the educational situation within a family. Needless to say, we fixed most of our attention on this particular aspect. It was shown once more that these children are doing quite well in the families. Yet, we should like to call attention to some very remarkable facts. Children that were neglected during a relatively short period of time (some months) clearly suffer from the negative effects of this situation, not to mention those that were neglected over a longer period of time. This can be gathered from various problems of adaptation during the first months after placement within the family. In some cases, these problems may prove very stubborn. Adoptive parents should be on the look out for them, especially when the problems of behaviour occur among children that show various signs of neglect. Medical situation at the moment of arrival, a past history with little attention for and stimulation of the child, and an age of six months or older, may serve as broad guidelines for "neglect". The behavioural problems of these children should lead to extra care so as to prevent them from becoming permanent problems.

It happens relatively often that children that are slightly older at the moment of arrival, suffer from various problems. For instance, they find it hard to deal effectively with their own emotions and those of others. Other people's emotions, and especially those of their parents, sometimes do not get across to them while expressing emotions in a normal way themselves often proves much of a problem. As was to be expected, therefore, we were able to come up with various negative effects on the children's behaviour effects that have been established by previous research as well. The most important problems mentioned by the parents were: lack of concentration, taking things away, lying, being inaccessible, or acting very friendly with everybody (seemingly accessible).

This kind of problem is not equally prevalent in all families. Families with own children sometimes seem to have to contend with more problems, even if the children's ages at the moment of arrival are equal. If there is only one adopted child in a family this also seems to give rise to a less favourable prognosis. In this context we should once again stress the fact that we are dealing with global data here. Further research with in-depth analyses of family systems in various types of families and the situation of the child has yet to be carried out. This will allow us to gain a better insight into why placements in families with seemingly comparable children can work out so differently.

Whatever the case, we for our part, have become convinced of the fact that adoptive parents, particularly where it concerns children that are several months old, should prepare extremely well for their task as educator. Where upbringing is concerned, obtaining a child that is, for instance, six months old is not the same as giving birth to an own child. Parents ought to know much about the effects of neglect on the actions of a child of a particular age. They ought to some extent to have an eye for what can normally be expected of a child in a particular phase of its development. This would reduce the chance of the parents' requiring too much of their children with regard to behaviour as well as emotions. Rest and stability prove to be important for neglected children. Confronting the child with drastic changes such as moving to another house during the first years after its arrival often does not work out well. Yet, it goes without saying that adoptive parents do not have dramatic events (such as deaths and divorces) in their own hands. One should realize, however, that neglected adopted children may be hard hit by these changes. Sometimes, the child has to develop the basic feelings of security and trust from the very beginning onwards. For many parents this is far from simple. We repeat, therefore, that the general statement "adoptive parents help adoptive parents best", is very true. Other parents with similar experiences can give good advice on the manifold problems of neglected adopted children.

In spite of the various problems in the field of upbringing, that are mentioned by the parents in all openness, we have noticed that there is a good relationship between parents and children in practically all families. Although children that are older than six months at the moment of arrival sometimes have a difficult start, the bond between parent and child develops automatically in almost all families. This may indicate that the effects of neglect can be undone, at least in the social sphere, if the child is placed in a favourable educational situation. This actually is the case with many of our adoptive families. We denote this as the "surplus" of adoptive parents, whereby one should not forget that the adopted children are extremely wished for.

Protective factors, however, may also be present in the children themselves. As we have already said before, many of them probably possess a strong vitality and will to survive. They survived situations that would kill many other children.

Apart from the educational situation in the family, it is equally important to try and find out how the children perform at school. We investigated this via school records and socio-emotional behaviour.

On the whole, the children prove to be functioning well from a cognitive point of view, although some children have some trouble with arithmetic. On the whole, however, there is little cause for special care. Yet, if we direct our attention to the group of neglected children we find that the negative effects on the children's cognitive performance that were expected by us actually make themselves felt. Problems in the field of learning and concentration occur among these children far more often; they repeated a class more often and have to turn to special education more often.

Finally, if we consider the children's socio-emotional behaviour, the picture presented to us is remarkably positive. Our Thai children are doing better where social contact and attitude towards work are concerned than similar groups of Dutch children (classmates and a national reference group). In this respect, neglected children do not perform worse than other children, which is rather remarkable. This fits in with our theory that these children may possess extra willpower, energy and perhaps ambition. This may explain their great effort, positive attitude towards work and good contact with classmates.

Although all of this presents us with a favourable picture, we should moderate things to some extent. In some families that obtained a child that already was a few years old, serious family problems arose. These parents found themselves in serious educational trouble, just because they were so full of good will. Their effort for and involvement with the child left nothing to be desired. What was wrong with them, though, was that they were poorly or badly prepared, sometimes even ignorant. In the seventies, and sometimes even still, this was more likely to happen. Sometimes, adoptive parents start their adventure insufficiently prepared, in spite of the fact that nowadays the various risk factors receive much more attention.

APPENDIX

A. NOTES

PRELUDE

1. For this introduction we heavily and thankfully drew on the data gathered by Elze van den Hazel and Katja Strijbosch.
2. The Thai group counts 4 twins among its members.
3. The Phyathai Baby's Home in Bangkok and a home in Udon Tahni directed by missionaries.

CHAPTER 3

1. For an explanation see F. Buurmeyer and D. Hermans, "De Gezins Dimensie Schalen als hulpmiddel bij gezinsdiagnostiek", Tijdschrift voor Psychotherapie, jaargang 11, nr. 5, september 1985.
2. For a detailed discussion see J.N. Zaal, (1981). Handleiding schoolbeoordelingslijst Schobl. Groningen: Wolters-Noordhoff.

CHAPTER 4

1. BIA formulated some guidelines for the manner of placement: Children are not placed over or between children that are already present. A difference in age of about 2 years with children that are already present, is to be preferred. Only in exceptional cases does BIA place differently (for instance, in case of siblings)
2. At the moment of investigation (1984) our group of parents had been married for an average of 18.5 years (the average year of marriage being 1965). National divorce percentages for couples that married in 1965 and split up after 11 years or later are not available yet. Ten years after the date of marriage 5.5% had split up and 20 years after this date 12.6% had split up, an increase of 7.1%. Of the couples that married in 1965, 5.8% had split up 10 years later. Starting from a similar increase of 7.1%, the number of divorces after 20 years of marriage will be 12.9%. We estimate by means of extrapolation, that the percentage of divorces after 18.5 years of marriage will be 11.8. Because the number of divorces increases with the year of marriage, we round up this number to 12% (Source: Central Statistical Office, 1984).
3. We do not know how large this group is in the West. Percentages vary from 7 to 15. We were not able to obtain a reliable picture from data of the Central Statistical Office. The number of chosen childless is on the increase. The number of involuntarily childless is estimated to be 10%.

CHAPTER 5

1. Of about 700 children the ages were known. There is little reason to suppose that these "Amsterdam" data are not representative for all adopted children in Holland.
2. These are: up to 6 months, 7 months to 1 year, 1-2 years, 2 years and older.
3. There is a connection between health and later motor development. The better the start, the greater the chance that the child will be ahead.
4. There is some degree of overlap. Twelve of the 16 children that showed a

lag in physical development also were behind in motor development.

CHAPTER 6

1. Because in Holland adoption is possible for married couples only, we start with that group.
2. We chose the year 1970 because in that year, the number of adopted children reached a record height (since 1956, enactment of the adoption law). After 1969, the number of births reached a record height (247, 590) as well.
3. Up to 1973, judgment was passed (cumulatively) in 1382 adoption cases. We took 1972 because of the then maintenance term of 2 years before the judge could pass judgment in the adoption case.
4. Sometimes, data will be given about the 116 children, sometimes about the 88 parents. In order to avoid misunderstandings, we will often indicate the group by means of numbers.
5. These are now organized by workers of the Adoption Centre in co-operation with Worldchildren.
6. Since 1985, there have been 10 intermediary organizations in Holland. This may seem quite considerable for so small a country. However, this situation works out badly for a good organization of the preparation of adoptive parents and the manner of placement of the child. It is to be hoped that a quick introduction of the licence system will lead to a more unequivocal policy.
7. Comparing data from 2 different countries, gathered with a time difference of 20 years, is problematic. Perhaps the time difference causes the least problems, because the USA had an adoption law a century earlier and because adoption there centres upon local adoption. We furthermore are convinced of the fact that in Holland similar differences will be found between the 2 groups of adoptive parents.
8. The scale used in Holland will be analysed for uni-dimensionality and reliability.
9. Tested with Kendall's tau B. All p-values smaller than or equal to 0.05 are significant.
10. There was a connection between the variable "mutual contacts among adoptive parents" and the 3 indices that was similar to that of the A.D. scores, but only for the index "communication" was it significant. The latter seems consistent because both are contact variables. In the case of the other 2 indices, other variables influenced the scores to such an extent that the connection is less obvious.
11. The relations between the clusters "communication" and "trust" on the one hand, and "telling", discussing adoption with the adopted child, on the other, are more significant. The more "communication" and "trust" between parents and child, the more "telling".
    We suppose that the child's age influences this connection. If we consider the connection between "communication" and "telling" for the various age groups, we see that the connection is not significant for the age groups 5-7 years and 8-10 years. The connection remains positive, though. In the age group 11-15 years, the connection remains significant (p=0.05). The same goes for the connection between "trust" and "telling". This significance disappears in the 2 youngest age groups, but the connection remains positive. In the oldest age group the connection between "trust" and "telling" remains significant.

CHAPTER 7

1. F.A. Buurmeyer and P.C. Hermans are preparing a thesis on the function of the FDS as an aid in family diagnostics.
2. In determining the standardization of the FDS we started from a standard group of 341 parents. The standard group consists of families with children in secondary education. Hence, the children in this standard group are older than the Thai children. Because the children's ages are bound to influence the family system, differences between the standard group and the Thai group are to be expected.
3. From: "Adoptie uit de kinderschoenen", p. 136.
4. Unfortunately, comparison with the standard group was impossible, because the interrelation of the scales was not calculated for this group.

CHAPTER 8

1. For 6 children the SCHOAL was not filled in, or filled in incorrectly: 3 parents (4 children) would rather not draw the school into the investigation, 1 teacher did not consider filling in the SCHOAL useful, and 1 teacher filled in the list incorrectly.
2. The teacher was asked to fill in the SCHOAL for the first girl and the last boy of the alphabetical list of names of the class. This prevented any arbitrariness in the selection of the classmates.
3. For 7 children, the questionnaire was not filled in, or filled in too summarily: 3 parents (4 children) did not want to draw the school into the investigation, 1 teacher did not want to co-operate, and for 2 children the list was filled in too summarily.
4. The classifications according to problematic background and age at the moment of arrival partly overlap. This is due to the fact that we automatically assigned the children under 3 months to the group without problematic background. Apart from that, there proves to be a close connection between background and age at the moment of arrival. Children that are older than 6 months at the moment of arrival more often have a problematic background than younger children (p < 0.001).
5. On the basis of this rather remarkable difference as regards content, in the answers to 2 questions that are directed at the same aspect more or less, we think that one of the questions is not valid. The questions were: "Do you consider this child a poor-average-good pupil in comparison with its classmates?" and "Does this child have trouble with learning and/or concentration?" We are under the impression that the first question gives rise to too positive an opinion. One obviously tends to consider a child a good pupil rather quickly. Answers to the question as to whether the child has problems are less likely to be negative. We therefore consider this question more real and attach more value to the answers to this question.
6. The national percentage of children that have repeated a class differs for boys and for girls and for form. For boys of the first up to and including the sixth form: 5.2, 4.0, 3.2, 1.5, 1.3, 0.9% respectively and for girls: 3.3, 2.7, 1.7, 1.0, 0.9 and 0.7% respectively. The percentage of 2.2 mentioned in the text was calculated thus: the percentages of repeaters in the first up to and including the sixth form (boys and girls) were added up and divided by six. Most of the Thai children are in lower school and that is where the largest percentage of repeaters is found. Even if we take all of this into consideration, the percentage in the Thai group is above the national average.

CHAPTER 9

1. In our discussion we focus on statistically significant connections.
2. We are not referring to a distinction between normal children and so-called "structo-pathic" children (Kok, 1984). We consider our group of children as a whole. For structo-pathic adopted children the effects of family changes will be even more complicated.
3. To avoid misunderstandings: the group of children with a problematic background (42) is not the same as the group of children older than 6 months at the moment of arrival (42). There is considerable overlap between both groups. Twelve children under 6 months at the moment of arrival have a problematic past history. Twelve children older than 6 months at the moment of arrival are without a problematic past history.
4. Verhulst mentions 2.1% for children presented to assistance organizations over a period of 12 months before his investigation. We asked the parents whether they ever contacted help in the 8 years that they have been taking care of the child. This was the case with 13% of them.
5. The Behaviour list was not filled in for 1 child on account of certain family circumstances.

CHAPTER 10

1. On account of special family circumstances, sometimes a question was not answered for 1 or 2 children.
2. For 9% of the children mention was made of individual variants of attachment; the mothers of 10% of the children were unable to come up with examples.
3. This connection was only found among children that were younger than 1 year when they came to Holland.
4. 8% Mention individual expressions of attachment, 17% are unable to come up with examples. These 17% and the 10% of footnote 2 indicate that in actual practice some people find it extremely hard to answer the question as to how their child shows its affection in daily life.

CHAPTER 11

1. Dr. H.A. Polman and N.S. Sorgedrager (M.A.) are paediatricians at the Diakonessen- and Roman Catholic Hospital in Groningen respectively. Both have been leading a national investigation into the medical conditions of arriving adopted children for some years now. Dr. T.W.J. Schulpen, paediatrician, Hospital Overvecht in Utrecht, is specialized in tropical diseases, and medical adviser of BIA.

B. BIBLIOGRAPHY

- Ainsworth, M.D., Blehar, M.C., Waters, E., Wall, S. (1978) *Patterns of attachment*. Hillsdale (NJ): Erlbaum.
- Bagley, C. Young, L. (1979). The identity, adjustment and achievement of transracially adopted children: a review and an empirical report, in: Verna, G., Bagley, C. *Race, education and identity*, London: Mc Millan.
- Boszormeny Nagy, I. (1973). *Invisible Loyalties*. Hagerstown Maryland: Harper Row.
- Bowlby, J. (1983). *Verbondenheid*. Deventer: Van Loghum Slaterus.
- Brodzinsky, D.M., Schechter, D., Braff, A. (in print). Children's knowledge of adoption: development, changes and implications for adjustment, in: Ashmore, R., Brodzinsky, D.M., *Thinking about the family: views of parents and children*. Hillsdale (NJ): Erlbaum.
- Bunjes, L.A.C., De Haan, A. (1983). Ja.... als we dat hadden geweten... (helaas, een receptenboek bestaat niet!), in: *Adoptie uit de kinderschoenen*. Deventer: Van Loghum Slaterus.
- Bunjes, L.A.C. (1980). Ontwikkeling van buitenlandse adoptiefkinderen: ervaringen op de kleuterschool, in: Hoksbergen, R.A.C., Walenkamp, H., *Opgroeidende adoptiefkinderen*, Deventer: Van Loghum Slaterus.
- Bunjes, L.A.C., Metman, A.H. (1986). In voorbereiding. Utrecht: Adoptiecentrum.
- Buuren, J.A. van (1983). Schijnwerpers op adoptie, resultaten van onderzoek, in: *Adoptie uit de kinderschoenen*. Deventer: Van Loghum Slaterus.
- Buurmeijer, F.A., Hermans, P.C. (1985). De Gezins Dimensie Schalen als hulpmiddel bij gezinsdiagnostiek, in: *Tijdschrift voor Psychotherapie*, jrg. 11, 5.
- Engeland, H. van (1986). *De ontdekking van het oppervlak*. Oratie, Utrecht: Rijksuniversiteit te Utrecht.
- Fanshel, D. (1972). *Far from the reservation*. Metuchen (NJ): Scarecrow Press.
- Feigelman, W., Silverman, A.R. (1983). *Chosen children: new patterns of adoptive relationship*. New York: Praeger.
- Garmezy, N., Rutter, M. (red) (1983). *Stress, coping and development in children*. New York: Mc Graw-Hill Book Company.
- Gill, O., Jackson, B. (1983). *Adoption and race*. London: St. Martin's Press Inc.
- Hägglund, G. (1980). *Att Adopteras*. Stockholm: Gotab.
- Hoksbergen, R.A.C. (red), Bunjes, L.A.C., Baarda, B., Nota, J.A. (1979, 1982). *Adoptie van kinderen uit verre landen*. Deventer: Van Loghum Slaterus.
- Hoksbergen, R.A.C., Walenkamp, H. (1980). *Opgroeiende adoptiefkinderen*. Deventer: Van Loghum Slaterus.
- Hoksbergen, R.A.C., Walenkamp, H. (1983). *Adoptie uit de kinderschoenen*. Deventer: Van Loghum Slaterus.
- Hoksbergen, R.A.C. (1985). *Een nieuwe kans*. Adoptie van Nederlandse en buitenlandse pleegkinderen. Oratie, Utrecht: Rijksuniversiteit te Utrecht.
- Hoksbergen, R.A.C., Loenen, A.B.M. (1985). Adoptie en attachment, in: *Kind en Adolescent*, jrg. 6, 2.
- Jackson, B. (1976). *Family experiences of inter-racial adoption*. London: ABAA.
- Jaffee, B., Fanshel, D. (1970). *How they fared in adoption*. New York:

Columbia University Press.
- Jewett, C.L. (1978). *Helping children cope with separation and loss*. Massachusetts: The Harvard Common Press.
- Kirk, H.D. (1953). *Community sentiments in reaction to child adoption*. Unpublished Ph.D. dissertation, Cornell University.
- Kirk, H.D. (1964, 1984). *Shared fate. A theory of adoption and mental health*. New York: Free Press.
- Kirk, H.D. (1981). *Adoptive kinship, a modern institution in need of reform*. Toronto: Butterworths.
- Kok, J.F.W. (1984). *Specifiek opvoeden*. Amersfoort: Acco.
- Loenen, A.B.M. (1984). *Attachment nader bekeken*. Intern rapport. Utrecht: Adoptiecentrum.
- Mansvelt, H.F.M. (1967). *Adoptiefouders aan het woord*. Alphen aan den Rijn: Samson.
- Meyer, R.W.J. (1975). Gedragsbeoordelingen door onderwijzers, in: *Pedagogische Studiën* (52).
- Nota, J.A. (1960). *Adoptie, hoe kunnen wij een kind aannemen?* Haarlem: De Toorts.
- Olson, D.H., Sprenkle, D.H., Russell, C.S. (1979). Circumplex model of marital and family systems: I. Cohesion and adaptability dimensions, family types and clinical application, in: *Family Process*. 1979,18,2.
- Olson, D.H., Russel, C.S., Sprenkle, D.H. (1983). Circumplex of marital and family systems: VI. Theoretical update, in: *Family Process*. 1983, 22, 69-83.
- Olson, D.H., Hamilton McCubin, J. (1983). *Families. What makes them work*. Beverly Hills: Sage Publications.
- Rathbun, C., McLaughlin, H., Bennet, Ch., Garland, J.A. (1965). Later adjustment of children following radical separation from family and culture, in: *American Journal of Orthopsychiatry*, 1965, 35, p.605.
- Rapport van de Werkgroep Adoptievoorbereiding Buitenlandse Pleegkinderen. Ministerie van Justitie (1978). Rapport Boeke, Den Haag: Staatsuitg.
- Raynor, L. (1970). *Adoption of non-white children. The experience of a British adoption project*. London: George Allen & Unwin.
- Riksen-Walraven, J.M.A. (1983). Mogelijke oorzaken en gevolgen van een (on)veilige eerste gehechtheidsrelatie, in: *Kind en Adolescent*, jrg.4,1.
- Rutter, M. (1979). *Verwaarlozing van jonge kinderen*. Utrecht: Het Spectrum.
- Skeels, H.M. (1966). Adult status of children with contrasting early life experiences. *Monographs of the Society for Research in Child Development*, 1966, 31,3.
- Sorosky, A.D., Baran, A., Pannor, R. (1975). Identity conflicts in adoptees, in: *American Journal of Orthopsychiatry*, 1975, 45, 18-27.
- Sorosky, A.D., Baran, A., Pannor, R. (1978). *The adoption triangle*. New York: Anchor.
- Stibane, K.W.U.F. (1983). Aspecten van kinderpsychiatrische problematiek bij adoptie van buitenlandse kinderen, in: *Adoptie uit de kinderschoenen*. Deventer: Van Loghum Slaterus.
- Thomas, A., Chess, S. (1980). *The dynamics of psychological development*. New York: Brunner/Mazel.
- Tizard, B. (1977). *Adoption: a second chance*. London: Open books.
- Tizard, B., Rees, A. (1977). A comparison of the effects of adoption, restoration to the natural mother, and continued institutionalization on the cognitive development of four-year-old children, in: *Child Development*, 1974, 45, 99-104.
- Triseliotis, J. (1973). *In search of origins*: The experiences of adopted

people. London: Routledge and Kegan Paul.
- Verhulst, F.C. (1985). *Mental health in dutch children*. Dissertatie, Rotterdam: Erasmus Universiteit.
- Walenkamp, H. *Maandblad voor de geestelijke volksgezondheid*, 5-1984.
- Wereldkinderen kwartaalblad, 1984, 3.
- Winick, M., Meyer, K.K., Harris, R.C. (1976). Malnutrition and environmental enrichment by early adoption, in: *Science*, 19-12-1976, p. 1173-1175.
- Yarrow, L.T. (1965). Theoretical implications of adoption research, in: *Perspectives on adoption*, Child Welfare League of America.
- Yarrow, L.T. and Goodwin, M.S. (1973). The immediate impact of separation: Reactions of infants to a change in mother figure. In L.J. Stone, H.T. Smith, and L.B. Murphy (Eds.), The competent infant: Research and commentary (pp. 1032-1040). New York: Basic.
- IJzendoorn, M.H. van (1979). Operationaliseringsproblemen bij onderzoek naar de affectieve relatie tussen ouders en kind, in: *Pedagogische Studiën*, 56, 358-368.
- IJzendoorn, M.H. van, Tavecchio, L.W.C., Goossens, F.A., Vergeer, M.M. (1982). *Opvoeden in geborgenheid*, Deventer: Van Loghum Slaterus.
- Zaal, J.N. (1978). *Sociaal-emotioneel gedrag in de klas*. Groningen: Wolters-Noordhoff.

C. TASKS AND COMPOSITION OF THE ADOPTION CENTRE

Research and teaching.
The Adoption Centre carries out research into the problems of adaptation of adopted children from various countries, motives of adoptive parents, causes of problematic placements and factors that influence the attachment between parents and child. Since 4-12-1984, there is a special chair for adoption. There are arrangements for higher education in this field. These arrangements are being developed.

Information and Consultation.
The Adoption Centre fulfils these tasks by organizing lectures at home and abroad, by making reports on subsidiary subjects, by making films and by sitting on committees dealing with adoption.

Educational Assistance.
The special character of the many tasks and the lengthy and intensive involvement with adoption helped the workers of the Adoptive Centre to build up specific knowledge about the special problems in adoption families. Before anything else, the Adoption Centre is a research institute. Parents with educational problems that need assistance will be referred to expert assistance organizations within their own region. For this purpose, a broad network of contacts has already been set up. If in the region no effective assistance is available, the Adoption Centre will undertake this task.

Composition
- René Hoksbergen,   – general co-ordinator, professor in the field of adoption of Dutch and foreign foster children; social psychologist/pedagogue
- Lucile Bunjes,   – assistance co-ordinator, remedial pedagogue
- Anthon de Vries,   – researcher of linguistic competence, clinical pedagogue
- Rob Lubbers,   – assistance adviser, professor of clinical educational theory, psychologist
- Femmie Juffer,   – researcher of the attachment relation adoptive parent-child, adaptation of Thai adopted children; clinical pedagogue
- Lieke Metman,   – researcher attachment relation, adaptation of adopted children from Mauritius; clinical pedagogue
- Isolde Andoetoe,   – researcher attachment relation; developmental psychologist
- Berte Waardenburg,   – researcher out of doors placement of foreign adopted children, adaptation Thai adopted children; clinical pedagogue
- Jacqueline Spaan,   – researcher out of doors placement of foreign adopted children, adaptation of adopted children from Mauritius; clinical pedagogue
- Ingrid Cauwels,   – researcher out of doors placement of foreign adopted children; clinical pedagogue
- Petra Flad,   – researcher of the development of Indian children of 9-11 years in local as well as intercountry adoption; clinical pedagogue
- Anny de Vries,   – social worker, clinical psychologist
- Ciska van Dijk,   – secretary
- Henk Broekzitter,   – secretary

THE AUTHORS

René Hoksbergen (21-9-1940) is married and has 2 children. He studied, among others, Social Psychology and Social Pedagogics at the University of Amsterdam (1962-1967). He obtained his doctorate with a thesis on "Profile of the Evening Secondary School Student" (1972). At present, he is professor in the field of "Adoption of Dutch and foreign foster children" at Utrecht University. He held and still holds various posts in the fields of teaching (policy adviser of the Minister of Education and Science) and adoption. He is general director of the Adoption Centre of the Social Faculty of Utrecht University. He appears in print a great deal, thereby focusing on problems in adoption, often gives lectures at home and abroad, and advises adoptive parents with family problems.

Femmie Juffer (22-10-1950) is married and has 2 children. She studied Clinical Pedagogics at Utrecht University (1969-1976). She held and still holds various executive posts within an adoption organization. At present, she is working for the Adoption Centre of Utrecht University and the Developmental Psychology Department of Leiden University. Is chief researcher of the Experimental Longitudinal Research into the educator-child interaction. Is preparing a thesis in the field of adoption. Gives lectures on adoption and guides adoptive families.

Berte C. Waardenburg (14-7-1958) studied Clinical Pedagogics at Utrecht University (1977-1983). Undergraduate thesis "Transfer of Foreign Adopted children". Now working as scientific researcher and social worker at the Adoption Centre of Utrecht University. At present, carrying out research into the causes of out of doors placements of foreign adopted children.